Create the Life of Your Dreams

Bob Kiser

Acknowledgements

When they say it takes a village, I'm pretty sure they were speaking to the creation of this book. Some of these people specifically assisted with this book, others in developing me as a person.

For being there at the right time to encourage me, I thank Francisco Fuentes, Shane Mayson, Ross Mondschain, Jason Phoebus, Denise McGowan, Gay Gelman, Martin Hurm, Warren Matson, Lynda Shadrake, Joy Loverde and Jeff Thomas.

As my father says, education is never wasted. Thanks to iPEC coaching school and Mr. Parmantie, my high school writing teacher. Now I appreciate all the revisions you made me do!

I would not be the man I am without my friends. Thank you Dianne Guarniello, Kari Keillor, Jane Noles, Alex Snook and Vern Magsino.

I am especially grateful for the people who read through different versions of my manuscript, offering their expertise and love. Thanks to Agustin Angel, Michael Corley, Max Anderson, Sara Maddox Johnson, Mike Kopplin and the best aunt in the world, Bess Reed.

This book never would have been started much less completed if it weren't for the team at Opus/Phoenix publishing. Their question, "Have you ever thought about writing a book?" started this entire process. Thanks to Gerald Farinas and Dane Tidwell. And special thanks to Lorelei Nikkola, editor extraordinaire.

As I express in my book, mentors are necessary to create the life of your dreams. I actually credit mine for saving my life. Thank you Leslie Reambeault and Dave Walsh for teaching me love and kindness as a way of life.

Thanks to the team at the Graham Clinical Performance Center at the University of Illinois. My appreciation for your continued support and willingness to listen to my ideas is without bounds.

By far my biggest appreciation and gratitude are for my parents, George and Martha Kiser. Without them, I really don't know where I would be or if I would even be. An extra thanks to George Kiser for all the time he took with this project. He read every version, offering his edits and encouragement every step of the way. You were right. I could do it.

Finally, I want to thank my clients. Each one of you taught me so much on our journeys together.

Table of Contents

There is a freedom waiting for you, on the breezes of the sky,

And you ask, "What if I fall?"

Oh, but my darling, What if you fly?

~Erin Hanson.

CHAPTER 1 – COMMITTING TO CHANGE

> *"I want a new life," my client told me at our first session.*
>
> *"I'm not really sure how I got here. When I was younger, I remember having passion! I couldn't wait to wake up. I was going to be a great artist. I know, it was a silly dream but I worked at my art day and night. I even managed to scrape enough money together to go to Europe to study. God, I can't remember a time that I felt more alive!*
>
> *Then real life happened. I took a job to pay the bills. I mean, I like real estate but I don't love it. It provides a great living. I guess I should just be grateful I have a job.*
>
> *Yet, I have this nagging feeling in my gut that I am meant to be doing more. I'm not sure if art is what I want to do, but I do know I want that kind of passion back in my life.*
>
> *I want my dream life..."*

I am going to make an assumption. You aren't completely happy with your life. How do I know? You've picked up this book.

I'll also make another assumption. You have at least some willingness to try to make your life better. Why do I say that? Well, you actually started *reading* this book.

Congratulations!

I can almost hear you saying, "Come on. Congratulations? Give me a break. I haven't done anything."

Actually you have. You have made it further than most.

I would venture to say many people feel the way you do. They aren't completely happy with their life. They know they were meant for something bigger, something deeper, yet they don't know what it is.

Sadly, that's where these people stop. They choose to go back to their known, safe life.

You have, instead, had the guts to pick up a tool that can help you. So congratulations on taking one step more than most.

There are some additional requirements, however, to create the life of our dreams. It takes fearlessness. It takes work. It takes a very brave soul.

DREAM LIVES

People are living their dream lives every day. They are successful. They are peaceful. They are happy.

Who are "these people?" They are those who embrace their dreams and won't settle for anything less. They look at life as one big adventure. Taking risks excites them. They feel the fear and create their success in spite of it.

Almost everyone is capable of creating the life of his or her dreams. And while most people like the idea of creating their dream lives, most rarely have enough desire to make it happen. Their biggest obstacle is lack of motivation. Well, motivation and not believing they deserve to succeed.

For years, I was jealous of other people. They were getting it all and I was stuck, spinning my wheels. I felt like I was on the outside looking in. After years of being "the guy who worked really hard but never quite got it" I realized I had chosen this role.

I didn't think I deserved success. When I got called back for that big Broadway musical, I froze, unable to dance. As I walked out, I could hear the casting associates expressing confusion. "He was so good at the first audition..." Though I felt bad, there was a certain amount of familiarity in this situation. I had fulfilled the role of the guy who *almost* gets things. Succeeding, getting what I wanted, was just not in my repertoire.

If I was going to get the life of my dreams, I had to be open to the possibility I might be good enough, deserving enough to get it. How open are you?

IS THIS BOOK FOR YOU?

I hate to waste time. Life is too short. Let's get to the point. Are you ready to create the life of your dreams? Are you ready to do what this book asks? Is this book for you?

Not sure? Then simply answer one question:

How happy are you with your life? On a scale from 1 – 10, with ten being 100% happy, rate your happiness:

> 10 – 8 = Awesome! Sounds like life is going great! Keep on keeping on. This book will probably reiterate a lot of things you already know. It would be a nice refresher for you and, at the very least, provide a new perspective.
>
> 7 – 5 = You are pretty happy with your life, but you know you want more. The question is, how willing are you to do the work? This book can help you, by adding more skills and ideas to your already impressive repertoire of success traits.

4 – 2 = You aren't happy with your life. What a great place to be! Why? It means that you probably have enough pain, enough desire, to work really hard at building a better life. That is IF you decide to do it. If you choose to do the work, this book will most likely change your life.

If you scored a 1, this book may not be for you at the moment. Why? I associate a 1 with hopelessness and depression. If this is you, I suggest you take another step before moving forward with the book. This book is about the use of coaching techniques to create a better life. Coaching is not appropriate in solely treating clinically depressed people or other types of mental illness. A mental health professional should help you address and move beyond the clinical issues that are holding you back. Then, I fully endorse coming back to this book and creating the life you deserve!

If you have decided this book is for you, the next question is will it change your life? I need to be honest with you. Your success will be directly proportional to your desire to get out of the discomfort or pain you feel in your current life and your willingness to do the work prescribed in the following pages.

We are creatures of comfort. If we are comfortable, we most likely won't change. And, really, why should we? It's only when the thought of "living one more day with what is not working" becomes more painful than the thought of "working hard to change" that we move forward.

Simply put, if you want more and are willing to work hard to get more, then this book is for you!

What's it worth to you to create the life of your dreams?

WHO AM I?

That is the question I would be asking if I were you...

I was born in Central Illinois to Robert and Shirley Wince. My mother had one daughter, Alicia, from a previous marriage. When Alicia was 11, her father took his life. My mother then married my father who had just come back from the army. From what I understand, one of the few things they had in common was their love of drinking. When I was three, she died from leukemia, leaving my sister and me with my father. A few months later, my sister bolted. Then it was just me with my alcoholic father.

My life was clearly not off to a great start. But that same year, something happened that changed my life forever. When my father would pass out from drinking, I would knock on the doors of other tenants in our building. One fateful day, I knocked on the door of George and Martha Kiser. They had just moved into the apartment across the hall and I grew to love going over to their place.

Pretty soon, Martha began baby-sitting me when my father had to work, or when he was busy drinking. As the years went by, his alcoholism progressed and I began to stay with George and Martha more and more. It felt like they were my parents in every way except legally.

When I was 15, George and Martha adopted me. I became Bobby Kiser. At that time, I thought it was the happiest day of my life. I mean, I knew it was *supposed* to be.

Actually it was the hardest day of my life. I loved George and Martha and wanted to be their son but I didn't want to let go of my father. I knew that staying with my dad meant my life would be in jeopardy but it was a life I had grown accustomed to. I was devastated by the fact that he so readily agreed to my adoption.

About the time of the adoption, something happened that changed my life forever. A trusted adult sexually abused me. Since this man was a highly respected person in our community, I felt the need for silence and blamed myself.

My life became filled with secrets and role-playing. I felt like I needed to act happy and not let the pain show. During this time I also had figured out that I was gay. All around me, people hated "the gays." I knew that coming out was not an option. I learned to be the Bobby I needed to be to make people happy.

I was not going to let my past dictate my future. I was going to be a Broadway star. After graduating from college, I jumped into the world of musical theater. At first, all was well. I was getting cool parts, touring with musicals I loved and living the life I thought I wanted.

Then I hit a wall. Auditions were not going well. I lost my confidence. Overall, life didn't feel good. I thought it was a slump- that I just needed to let off steam.

I started drinking and doing drugs. I believed my motive was simply to have fun. Some years later, a therapist helped me see I was self-medicating to feel better. No matter who I thought I was, deep down I was still that little boy who had not dealt with his past. I became overwhelmed and went into a severe depression that included thoughts of suicide.

At that point, I sought help. I started dealing with a past I had tried to outrun. I started looking at the secrets I had kept even from myself.

I was the child of an alcoholic, gay and a survivor of sexual abuse. I had a lot to process. My therapist helped me to be honest with myself, to start loving all aspects of myself (even the ones I didn't like) and, most importantly, taught me to forgive myself. I learned that, though I did things I wasn't proud of, I was doing the best I could with the tools I had.

After a couple of years of working with my therapist and seeking support for my addiction issues, I was stable and ready to start creating a life I loved. I just wasn't quite sure what that life looked like.

What I did know was I didn't want to be an actor. I had spent years trying to be someone else, both onstage and off, because I hated who I was. No more. I only wanted to be me. No more being someone different to fit in or make people happy.

So the question I had to start asking myself was, "Who am I?"

I began to do the work you will find in this book. I knew I wanted to help people. Many amazing people had, literally, saved my life and I wanted to give back. I wanted to help people who experienced the same fears, the same chaos I had, and to show them things really can be ok.

I thought about becoming a therapist. Though I loved the work I did in therapy, I didn't feel like that was a fit. Because I loved the spiritual journey I had taken, I thought about becoming a minister. But, as much as I love talking about spiritual principles, I have no desire to tell people what to think about God or whatever they worship.

One of my friends told me that I was really good at starting things. While most people fear the new and unknown, I thrive on it. At this point, I had already started two nonprofit organizations. My friend said just watching me made him tired. I was often juggling at least three different projects, usually in a leadership position. I seemed to be an expert at organizing things.

Finally, someone suggested I try life-coaching school. George had instilled in me the notion that any class is a good investment. Even if I didn't become a coach, I would still have the education.

On the very first day of class, I knew I was home. As a coach, I would be able to help people create the life *they* wanted, helping them identify and clarify their goals. Life coaches inspire clients into action by connecting their goals to their inner passions and values. Along the way, coaches walk their clients through obstacles and fears, to remind them they really can be successful.

And my favorite part of the job - we get to celebrate with our clients when they are successful!

It's about helping clients remember they have choices. Often, when we get overwhelmed with life, we forget this immutable fact. We think we have no choice but to keep doing what we are doing.

If you gain nothing else from this book, please know, embrace and never forget that *you always have a choice*. The choice may be only in the way you view the situation, but there is always a choice. *Always.*

INGREDIENTS FOR MAKING CHANGE

"Without change, something sleeps inside us, and seldom awakens. The sleeper must awaken." - Frank Herbert

When prospective clients come to me wanting to change, I warn them that it's not for the faint of heart. For serious change to occur, you will need three key ingredients. If even one is missing, there will probably be no significant change, or you will be unhappy with the change that does occur.

1. *HONESTY:* What do you want, really want? Not what your parents want. Not what your friends think you should want. Not even what society dictates you should want. Do you have the guts to say "yes" to yourself and your values and "no" to everything else? How honest can you be about your strengths and weaknesses? Do you have the guts to admit when you are wrong or need to work on something in order to move forward? Any goal built on dishonesty with yourself rests on a faulty foundation. Even if you become outwardly successful, inside you will probably be unhappy.

2. *OPEN-MINDEDNESS:* It's always amusing when people say they dislike their current life but are close-minded about trying new things. If you are going to change your life, you must be open to new possibilities. Now, this doesn't mean every suggestion is right for you. It does mean no automatic veto of possible solutions. One must have a willingness to say something like, "That's new to me. Tell me more…" By learning about new things, your repertoire of goals to include in your new life increases, as well as the means to obtain them.

3. *WILLINGNESS:* To change your life, you must be willing to:
   - Try
   - Make mistakes
   - Take the next step forward
   - Look for solutions when there doesn't seem to be any.

Willingness is the intent to act. It is the precursor to action. If you want to create the life of your dreams but don't have the willingness to do the work, you will continue with your present life.

ACTION

I know many people who brag about reading self-help books. Armed with new ideas, they love discussing what's possible. They seem to have the willingness to do the work. In fact they're always ready to take that next step… tomorrow.

Your life won't change by simply reading this (or any) book. If you are going to change, you must take action. Period. What most separates those who succeed from those who fail is that the successful take action to make their dreams come true.

EXERCISE #1- Willingness meter

How willing are you to take action to create the life of your dreams?

Circle your level of willingness

1   2   3   4   5   6   7   8   9   10

Not willing   Completely willing

If your willingness is 7 or above move on to the next section...

If your willingness is less than 7, answer the following question:

When you have obtained the life of your dreams, how will you feel? Using the table on the next page, circle the feelings that would apply.

admired	content	fortunate	kind	reassured
alive	courageous	free & easy	liberated	rebellious
at ease	daring	glad	loved	re-enforced
attractive	delighted	gleeful	loving	relaxed
blessed	determined	good	lucky	rich
bold	dynamic	grateful	optimistic	satisfied
brave	eager	great	overjoyed	serene
bright	ecstatic	happy	peaceful	sure
calm	elated	hopeful	playful	surprised
certain	encouraged	important	pleased	tenacious
cheerful	energetic	impulsive	positive	thankful
clever	enthusiastic	inspired	prosperous	thrilled
comfortable	excited	interested	provocative	understood
confident	festive	joyous	quiet	wonderful

After considering how you would feel if you did obtain the life of your dreams, how has your willingness changed?

HOW TO USE THIS BOOK

This book is about the process of creating the life of your dreams. Though as a coach, I never tell anyone the right way to do something, I have found there are commonalities for most clients who succeed. The following pages contain my experiences, both personally and as a coach. The stories I use are from actual cases but the names and some details have been changed to protect anonymity.

This book also contains exercises, which should help clarify the information. They are helpful in applying what you've learned to your own life. Do the exercises as you read, and you'll get a lot more out of it. I have also found that going back to the exercises after a period of time can be helpful and often leads to further insights.

Be gentle with yourself and trust the process. When coaches say, "trust the process," they mean there will be times when it appears there is no solution. When this occurs, my clients usually become discouraged. But as a coach, I get excited. Why? I have been there before. I know this is the moment to let go of what's "supposed" to be, to make room for what *could* be. During such moments, our brain, like a computer pausing to load the next screen, put us "on hold" while it creates new ideas. It's about getting comfortable with the pause and not aborting the creation before it comes to fruition.

This book is about creating your dream life, not stressing about it. Don't use this as another tool to beat yourself up. During the process, dedicate yourself to love instead of fear, positive feelings instead of negative. Be open to mistakes, as they will happen. It might get messy. Let it. Be open to the fact that you probably will think differently after this book. Embrace it.

Oh, and the last thing: Don't forget to have fun!

So are you ready? Sign this contract with yourself, and let's begin...

I, _____,
am ready to change. In this process, I
promise to be:

- as HONEST as I can be with myself

- OPEN to new ideas

- WILLING to take risks and try new things

Above all, I will be gentle with myself and
have FUN in the process!!!

Signature:

CHAPTER 2 – DISCOVERING WHAT YOU REALLY WANT

Rob (Part 1)

"I don't know what I want to be when I grow up."

Those were Rob's words during our first session. He was a successful dean of a small college. Though he had made a career of academics, he felt it was never really his passion.

Since Rob was retiring, he thought this was his chance to create the life of his dreams. He believed that the only reason he had not done so before was out of duty to his parents and family.

In the weeks to come, we discovered that without the parameters of what he thought he should be, he didn't know who he was. Our journey was re-discovering who he was, and thus, what he wanted.

He had to remember how to dream the impossible...

WHAT DO YOU WANT?

Though it may sound obvious, the first thing you must do to create the life of your dreams is figure out what you want. Many people have no idea just what that is. They only know they want something better than what they have now. They float through life, too afraid to claim their passions, their authentic lives. Probably the number one reason people seek my services is to clarify their life purpose. They aren't happy. They have the feeling they are meant for more, but don't know what. They say they feel like they are spinning their wheels, never really getting ahead. Makes sense they aren't moving ahead when they don't know what "ahead" looks like.

Many of my clients think they are lazy. They say they just need to work harder, but usually this is not the case. It's lack of clarity. When people claim their dreams, their authentic selves, they actually start to have the opposite problem, they find they need to remember to stop and rest. Their life becomes so exciting they just want to do more to create their visions.

So what do you want? That is the question. By the way, I love this part of the process. Why? Anything is possible! Exploring what you *really* want is about playing. Nothing is wrong at this stage. In fact the more "outside the box" you can think the better.

When a client says to me *"I know this is really crazy but I think what I really want is...,"* I know she has struck gold. It's in those "crazy" thoughts that we usually find our truest selves.

As a coach, my task is not to judge a client's goals as "right" or "wrong". My job is to listen and make sure their goals are in alignment with their authentic selves. The hardest part of my job is getting clients to claim their dreams. If clients can't get specific in what they want, then no matter how hard they work, they will probably continue to have that nagging feeling that something is wrong.

Many of us don't claim our dreams because we are scared to death. Scared we might not achieve our dreams. Scared we don't deserve them or that we aren't talented enough. Scared of what people will think of us if we don't succeed. Scared of what people will think of us if we *do* succeed. Scared to have faith and believe.

Jim came to me because he felt like he was standing still in his life. I asked what he wanted most. He began telling me his dreams, what he most desperately wanted, but then he suddenly stopped. Stuttering, Jim retracted what he had just said. He might have wanted those things at one time but he knew they were foolish. He was wiser now. Jim didn't believe in childish dreams anymore.

"Too bad," I thought. I wish he still did.

You see, it's in childish dreams that passion and possibility are found. Sometimes we grow up too much for our own good.

As children, knowing what we want is so easy. For the most part, children don't judge their desires. They just know they want something. Period. One moment they want to play superheroes. Suddenly the backyard is a bustling metropolis and they're out to save a damsel in distress. An hour later, they want to be an astronaut, and their lawn is a never-ending space full of stars, planets and aliens. And this is expected. It is ok for children to be creative, to live in fantasy. No judgment is required, in fact, they're being cute.

But something changes. We are all expected to grow up. Pretty soon the dreaming, which seemed so much fun as a kid, becomes a liability. We are told that we need to start being "realistic," we must act responsibly and stop being so selfish.

> *"Stop living in fantasy. Drawing won't pay the bills."*
> *"That might be fine as a hobby, but you have a family to support."*
> *"Its fine to play sports while you are young but you will have to get a real job. You should major in accounting."*

The first time we are mocked or shamed for our dreams, we may develop a block against imagining big lives for ourselves. Instead of a life fueled by our dreams and passions, we decide to choose a life of smallness. It makes us feel safe. Shame and fear begin to dictate the life we create.

When I was around 12 years old, I would spend hours in my backyard pretending I was performing on Broadway. I would sit with my dog Snoopy on a picnic table and serenade him for hours. He became well versed in all the latest musicals.

One summer I built a theater in the backyard. It was so cool! My dad helped me get the plywood for a proscenium to add to two big platforms I had for the stage. My mom made curtains with weights so they wouldn't blow in the wind. I even had lights with dimmers.

Did I mention it was SO cool?

That summer I was so happy, making up my shows and performing them for Snoopy. I was doing exactly what my soul wanted to do. I was fearless.

Then I went back to school.

"Hey Bobby, nice howling in your backyard! Are you gay or something?"

I was mortified. It hadn't even dawned on me that people could see my stage in the backyard. I just thought it was me and Snoopy.

After that, I took down my theater. I packed it away. Oh, I still thought it was cool, but that feeling was overshadowed by the feeling that I was a fool. I started getting overwhelmed with the fear of what people might think of me. My choices became centered on getting validation from others.

As a young actor in college, that little boy who was made fun of in his backyard, stayed with me. I always felt like I had to be perfect because I never knew who was watching or what they were thinking of me. This was hard because in order to be a great actor, it is almost guaranteed that you will look foolish at some point in your training. How else are you going to learn?

DREAMING VS REALITY

My client Jim was frustrated because he believed he had to be realistic in creating his dream life. Reality has a place in obtaining goals, but worrying about obstacles too soon can overwhelm us and make us abandon our dreams. Most people have a very effective internal guard that tells them their dreams are impossible even before they try. If one continues to allow it to express this view too soon in the process of creating his dream life, pretty soon that person will probably quit dreaming at all. If all dreams are impossible, why bother?

That's why one of my first questions in an initial coaching session is usually, "What would you be doing if it were impossible for you to fail?"

It addresses that internal guard by saying perhaps it isn't possible but what if you *could* succeed? Then what? I invite you to answer the question for yourself. Do you have the courage to admit what your dream life looks like?

"What would you be doing if it were impossible to fail?"
Write your answer below.

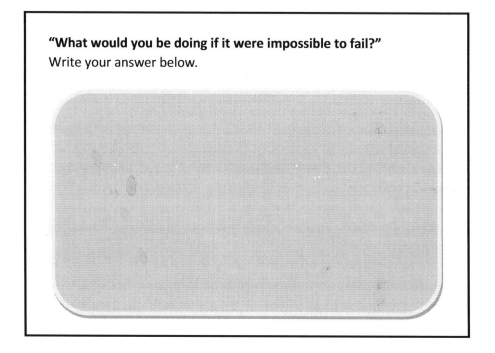

If answering this question was difficult or even overwhelming, be gentle with yourself. Be curious and explore *why* you are having difficulties identifying your dreams. What would happen if you did achieve your dreams? Do you have a fear about saying your dream out loud? If so, what is your biggest fear about writing down your dream? Once you have answered those questions, try again.

Still can't think of what you want? Be patient. If you are like most of us, you and/or society has beaten into yourself the improbability of achieving the big dreams. It takes time to let your guard down enough to dream. Just keep consistently asking yourself, "What is it I want?"

Give yourself permission to dream the impossible. Soon you will hear the answer. I promise.

SAFETY FIRST

Even as you read this, I bet some internal guards have already jumped in. Yes, it's all fine and good to daydream, but we must also think about putting food on the table, having a place to sleep, money for clothes, etc.

The internal guards are partly right: You do need to think about those things. I never recommend someone sacrificing safety for irresponsible goals. When clients are creating the life of their dreams, I suggest trying to keep the rest of their lives as stable as possible, for as long as possible. It's hard to dream of writing that next great novel when you aren't sure whether you will have a place to sleep. The more energy you expend just trying to survive, the less you have for dreaming big. And no matter how big or small a concern it must be addressed.

But right now is not the time. In fact, the more conscious of responsibility and worrying about what you *should* do, the more obstacles you will create for yourself.

Right now, any thought, any dream - no matter how crazy it seems - is ok. In fact the crazier the better.

Remember, we are in the "dreaming phase". By definition, it is just a thought. No action will be taken right now. There is no danger in dreaming. Not even in dreaming crazy or irresponsible things. Thank God!

As you read this chapter and do the exercises, every time you think, "That's not practical!" or "That would be totally irresponsible," say something like this to your internal guard:

"Thank you so much for telling me your concerns. I promise we will address them later but, right now, that is not helpful information. At this moment, I'm just dreaming, playing. I promise I won't make any decisions until I address your concerns."

EXERCISE #2- Dreaming big

If you could have anything, do anything, be anything, what would it be? Think big. This is not the time to be shy. What is the life of your dreams? Fill in your dream life for each category:

Career	
Home/Living Arrangements	
Relationships (Friends, family, intimate)	
Fun & Enjoyment	
Personal Development	
Spirituality	

Finding the exercise difficult? Try a different perspective:

You find a bottle on a beach. Accidentally rubbing the bottle, a magic genie pops out. For releasing him, the genie agrees to grant you three wishes. The only wish you can't make is for more wishes. What do you wish for?

Or

If you won the lottery and money was no object, what would you do?
What would be different in your life?

I presented the lottery question to a group of medical students enrolled in one of my seminars. These students were obviously very bright. They also were very conscious of trying to give the "right" answer.

"I would pay off my debt, help my family and buy a nice house," was the most common answer. Though not doubting these goals were important to them, I pushed them further.

"Really? That's it? You have won the lottery and have unlimited amounts of money. You would do nothing else?"

The students started shifting in their chairs nervously. Some looked around the room at their fellow classmates. Others looked down at their notes, probably hoping I wouldn't call on them.

One student, finally, spoke up and said those magic words I listen for, "This is going to sound crazy but..." and she went on to tell how she would love to have a recording studio. I expressed my excitement.

"Really? That sounds so cool. Tell me more."

She told us that she writes songs and would love to start recording them. Of course her inner critic popped up and told her (and us) that, of course, she could never do it. She chose medicine and that was that. I challenged her, saying that maybe she could do both. We went on to another exercise and finished the seminar in a few days.

Six months later, I received an email from her. She was excited to tell me she had written a song, copyrighted it, and won first place in a song-writing contest. She said just the opportunity to say her dream out loud in the seminar encouraged her to go for it.

EXERCISE #3- What do I want?

Free writing about a question creates opportunities for us to make discoveries about what we really think or want. Write 2 pages about:

- If you could take an all-expense paid, year-long sabbatical to do anything you wanted, what would you do?
- If it were possible to take a time machine and meet the future you, who do you think this person might be? Write about this person.
    - What are you doing?
    - What are your top 5 accomplishments?
    - What is a typical day in your life?

EXERCISE #4- That would be crazy!

List 10 exciting, crazy things that you would LOVE to try but couldn't actually imagine doing. If you don't have a feeling of excitement, nervousness or a pit in your stomach, you haven't reached the really crazy dreams. Remember, these are YOUR wildest dreams ~ not your mother's, not your partner's, not your boss's...

Examples:

> *Audition for the local theater group's next play*
> *Learn to play the tuba*
> *Buy a video camera and start making short films*
> *Learn to SCUBA dive and then book a trip to the Caribbean.*

1.
2.
3.
4.
5.
6.
7.
8.
9.
10.

HOW HAPPY ARE YOU?

When we aren't sure what we want, sometimes it's helpful to look at how fulfilled we are in different parts of our lives. Once we acknowledge where we aren't happy, then we can ask, "What would make me happy?"

On the next page is a fun exercise that can be quite insightful.

EXERCISE #5- Drive that car

Circle the number that reflects your satisfaction for each area of your life.

10 = Extremely Satisfied

1= Extremely Unsatisfied.

Health	Career	Self - Development	Finances	Social life	Intimate Relationships	Creative Expression
10	10	10	10	10	10	10
9	9	9	9	9	9	9
8	8	8	8	8	8	8
7	7	7	7	7	7	7
6	6	6	6	6	6	6
5	5	5	5	5	5	5
4	4	4	4	4	4	4
3	3	3	3	3	3	3
2	2	2	2	2	2	2
1	1	1	1	1	1	1

Now, for each column, color each box up to the number you chose:

Example
Health = 8
Career = 4
Self-Development = 7

Health	Career	Self-Development
10	10	10
9	9	9
8	8	8
7	7	7
6	6	6
5	5	5
4	4	4
3	3	3
2	2	2
1	1	1

Now imagine this is a road you are driving down. In the example, for "health" the car would be at one level and then it would hit the pothole called "career." This is how our life can feel when we have huge gaps between different areas of our life. Sometimes it's not so much about getting all 10s but rather striving for balance that brings happiness to our lives.

BONUS: For each area, think of one thing you might be able to do to raise your satisfaction level by one point. Make sure it is an action item that is doable and not overwhelming.

JEALOUSY

Sometimes when clients are not sure what they want, I ask them, "Who are you jealous of?" Why? By definition, these people have what we want (or think we want.) Usually we think, deep down, we are capable of achieving those things.

In sessions, I am usually listening not so much for the actual physical items clients want but rather the experience they are seeking. I find that some people want an experience they think others are having. Like wanting to be rich. It may not necessarily be the money they want but rather the feeling of being debt-free.

For example, Sam is jealous of Mike because of all his vacations. He thinks it's because Mike gets to go to exotic places. Sam doesn't have the money to travel like that. Sam says the solution is for him to make more money.

In reality, though, Sam is just yearning for a break from his busy schedule. He's stressed. Sam, deep down, wants rest and relaxation. By realizing he just needs some time off to decompress, he might find that taking a day off every once in a while helps. But if Sam had gone with his initial thought of "need to make more money," he might have added more stress, the one thing he ultimately wanted to avoid.

EXERCISE #6- Get Jealous

Who are you Jealous of?	Why?	Which of their experiences do you want?	What is one thing you are willing to do in order to achieve this goal?
Sam	On Facebook, he's always out doing things	I would love to see new places and meet new people.	I can start putting myself out there, committing to do one new social event a week.
			'

LIFE PURPOSE

Some people know from a very early age what they want to do with their lives. When this is the case, decisions are easier. Speeding toward a goal is simple when you know what the goal is. What about when we don't know the goal? What about when we don't know our life's purpose?

I have been on both sides of the fence. From an early age, I knew I was destined to be in Broadway musicals. When I made that discovery, a lot of decisions were geared towards that goal and I finally became a professional actor. Then, after doing it for awhile, I discovered I didn't want to be an actor anymore.

Wow, what a change! I encountered the most severe depression I could imagine. Without a purpose, my life seemed confusing and chaotic. I realized I had no idea what I wanted for a career. I was in a void.

When clients are stuck, when they aren't sure what they want, I suggest we look at their life's purpose. I pose these questions: Why do you think you were born? What do you need to accomplish before you die?

PERSONAL MISSION STATEMENT

Companies use mission statements to keep them on track. A mission statement declares why an organization exists and reminds it of its purpose. When companies start growing quickly or feel like they have lost their way, they can go back to their original mission statement to re-focus their efforts and provide clarity in moving forward.

People can create their own personal mission statements. It helps keep their overarching goal in mind at all times. It is especially helpful to clients who are very talented and can do many things. The obstacle for these individuals can be the uncertainty about where to concentrate their energies. When should they say "yes" and when should they say "no"? By creating a personal mission statement, they have a standard to weigh their choices against.

EXERCISE #7: Personal mission statement

Write down 2 or 3 things for each question.

    1. What is your purpose here on this planet?

    2. What skills do you possess that can help accomplish this purpose?

    3. What is one of your current big goals?

Now circle the best answer for each question. Using the numbers of each question, insert the circled answer into the appropriately numbered place in the statement below.

I am here to_____(1)_____. Using my skills of____(2)_____, I will_____(3)_____.

As an example, here is my mission statement:

I am here to partner with others to create the life of their dreams. Using my skills of leadership, empathy and compassion, I will speak to others in workshops and presentations on the concepts in this book.

I suggest that you periodically revisit this exercise to see how well you are living your mission statement. Are your choices reflecting the overall vision you have for yourself? If not, then maybe new choices are called for. And sometimes, as we change, we find that we need to revise our mission statement to reflect the new person we have become. Either way, our mission statement keeps us conscious of who we want to be.

A VISION FOR YOU

When people find out I'm a life coach, I am often asked to suggest a tool that might help them create a better life. Though there are many, one of my favorites is called a "vision board." It is simply a collection of pictures (usually cut from magazines) of things that you would like to have in your life.

Why a vision board? I have found it brings clarity, awareness and focus to clients. How? When reflected upon regularly, it keeps clients' goals in their consciousness. Also, just by looking at pictures and saying "yes" to some and "no" to others, they really are asking themselves, "What's important to me and what do I really want?"

The human mind loves to solve problems. In creating a vision board, you are saying to the mind, "Okay, here is what I want my life to look like...Go find it!" It activates the subconscious like no other coaching tool. If I have a client create a board, in two to four weeks I often hear, "You are never going to believe what happened. Remember how I put that picture on my board? Well, I got it!"

Some people believe that making a vision board activates the Universe (or the powers that be) to help create what they want. I have never seen any conclusive research that supports this claim. However, I made a vision board a couple of years ago and the result fascinated me.

For one section of my board, I chose pictures that reflected my desire to travel. I had not traveled extensively due to lack of funds. As I cut out the pictures, I was skeptical. How was putting pictures on a board going to allow me to travel more? But I did it anyway. I really wanted to test this tool.

Last year, a good friend started working for an airline and received a "family/friend" pass. The holder of this pass could fly, free of charge, on my friend's airline and some others. Out of the blue, he offered this pass to me.

This year I have flown nationally and internationally, two and sometimes three times a month. Someone remarked to me that it was neat that I had "unlimited opportunities to travel." That phrase sparked my memory. I remembered I had cut out that exact phrase, *"Unlimited Opportunities to Travel"* and put it on my board. And yes...I definitely had received it! I also put on my board, *"First Class Travel"* and a picture of an airline seat that converted into a bed. Two months ago, I was on an international flight with my pass, got bumped up to business class and found myself with a seat just like the picture.

EXERCISE #8: Vision board

1. Start going through magazines and cut out pictures of how you would like your life to be. The goal is to pick the pictures that give you a strong, positive emotional response. Also be on the lookout for the voice inside you that says *"I would like that but I could never have it."* If you hear that...CUT THAT PICTURE OUT!!! Those are definitely the kinds of things we want on your board.
2. Attach the pictures to a poster board, bulletin board or something of the sort.
3. Then put the board where you will see it every day.

I created mine a little differently than the process I described above. I used the Windows 7 Paint Program by copying and pasting pictures from the Internet to my "board." I then saved it as my "wallpaper" so every time I turn on the computer I see it.

Rob (Part 2)

Rob found it hard to let go of what he thought he "should" be in order to dream about what he "wanted" to be. As we talked, the running joke between us was his "BUT..." monster.

"So Rob, I hear you might want to go traveling through Europe next year?"

"Sure, but I couldn't possibly do that because..."

Soon we developed a "BUT-MONSTER-FREE" zone. Rob started to embrace coming up with "wild and crazy" ideas. When we were in a dreaming phase of development, the "BUT..." monster was not allowed. He was welcome to join us later when we started addressing obstacles.

Rob developed a vision and then created a doable action plan that addressed his obstacles.

And he eventually did what the "BUT..." monster thought was impossible: He took a trip to Europe.

CHAPTER 3 - THE "WHY"

Jim was a personal trainer who wanted to start a fitness center for families. It was an interesting idea and had a lot of potential. Seemed pretty easy to me.

Soon we hit a stumbling block. Jim wasn't doing his assignments in-between sessions. These were assignments we had created together from things he said he wanted to achieve. If I hadn't known better, I would almost have thought Jim wasn't interested in doing this project. To say the least, I was confused.

"Jim, my gut is telling me you don't want to create this fitness center."

"But Bob, if I did this I would be such a good guy."

Bingo! After a little more exploration, he revealed his family had suggested he start a fitness center. They had expressed how happy it would make them. Jim wanted to be good guy and to please his family but he didn't want to own a fitness center.

ASKING "WHY"

After you have a clear idea of how you want your life to look, I suggest you ask yourself, "Why do I want this life?" Is your motive to "fix" yourself or is it to "better" yourself?

Though at first glance the two may seem the same, there are subtle differences.

When one attacks a goal in order to fix oneself, there can be a feeling of negativity, as though you are broken. When people feel they have to fix issues just to be "ok", I believe they are motivated by fear.

The more fitting approach is creating a goal in order to "improve" yourself. In this scenario, you don't perceive yourself as bad but you do acknowledge that something different - and more effective - is possible and desired. The feeling I associate with this approach is *hope*.

Usually goals created in hope are more successful, more appealing than those springing from fear.

An Example: Two people are planning to attend medical school. Lindsey goes because she loves the thought of being a doctor. She wants to learn everything she can about medicine. Her ultimate goal is to cure cancer, to make a difference in the world. Sam goes to school because everyone in his family is a doctor. He is afraid if he doesn't go, he will be letting them down.

Put yourself in the shoes of both students. The desire to study would probably come easier to Lindsey because she is motivated by a deep passion. Though the studies may be hard, natural curiosity and interest will carry her through.

Sam, on the other hand, may feel anxious and depressed when he thinks about school. Studying would be harder for him because he is only doing it to make his family happy. He feels like he doesn't have a choice.

Another way to summarize the *why* of our two students is that Lindsey "wants to" become a doctor and Sam feels that he "has to" become a doctor.

WANT TO vs. HAVE TO

Finding the motivation for a goal you *want* to accomplish is so different from finding it for one you *have* to accomplish. To be more specific, people want a choice. Even if we don't like something, if we can feel like we are choosing it and not being forced to do it, then we usually can find motivation.

41

A huge part of my coaching job is to show clients they do have choices. They don't *have* to do anything. Yes, there are consequences for not doing certain things but we always have a choice. When clients tell me, "*I have to do…*" I ask them to brainstorm reasons that they might *want* to do the task instead of *having* to do it.

I suggest we re-frame "*I have to do…*" and change it to "I want to do it because…"

When you feel like you "have to" or you "should do" something, try remembering you always have a choice. When you get to a point where you are choosing to do something, then motivation is a little easier.

EXERCISE #9- Reframing *"HAVE TO"* into *"WANT TO"*

Change your own personal "have to's" using the chart below.

What I feel like I "have to" do	What might happen if I don't do it?	Choices	Re-frame to "want to" do	Feeling
I have to do my taxes	• Fines • Legal fees • Jail	• Do my taxes • Don't do my taxes • Do them later	I want to do my taxes because in the long run, I will avoid a lot of headaches. Plus I might be getting money back.	More willing, though not thrilled.

CREATING FROM OUR AUTHENTIC SELVES

Originality. Most of us applaud when we see it but are usually afraid to try it ourselves. It can be risky to be original. What will people say? If the wheel isn't broken, why fix it? It's probably just safer to do what we know.

As a coach, I want to make sure my clients are being true to themselves. Too often, I see them adopt others' values and beliefs without stopping to wonder if they really agree. It's almost like the "herd" mentality. Then they wonder why they aren't motivated to move forward.

We are more than the roles we play. Sometimes these roles can conflict with our core values.

Goals are easier to achieve and more fulfilling when we create from our authentic selves. Our authentic selves are our core that is made up of our most basic values. No matter what role we take in life, if we are in touch with our authentic self, it will come through in all situations.

But unfortunately, we forget our authentic selves, our true nature. Instead, we grow up to believe we are the sum of our many roles. But we are more than that. And sometimes these roles can conflict with our core values.

Joe is a top manager of a corporation. In this role, he has been told it is his job to get the Millers, low-income elderly people, out of their home. The corporation wants the land and that is that. So if he was just a manager, then his decision would be easy: Do as he is told.

Coming from his authentic self, though, this becomes difficult. In his heart of hearts, Joe believes he is here to help people. He actually started an organization that helps find reasonably priced homes for low-income families. Joe decides he needs to quit his manager job because the actions required don't fit who he is in his heart.

What is the danger of *not* being our authentic selves? Self-Sabotage.

We have enough obstacles. Why sabotage ourselves further because of the knowledge that, deep down, we are not being authentic? It's hard to see clients regret years of hard work accomplishing something that doesn't reflect who they truly are. Though maybe rewarding for a bit, living only for the validation of others and not acknowledging our authentic selves can eventually leave us feeling depressed and unfulfilled.

When we stop listening to ourselves and rely on the values of others, we run the risk of losing ourselves. It's hard for us to know what we really want. When we lose ourselves, we may start feeling dissatisfied and even resentful of those people who seem to know what they want.

But when we are aware of and acting from our authentic self, our experience is one of peace, contentment and happiness.

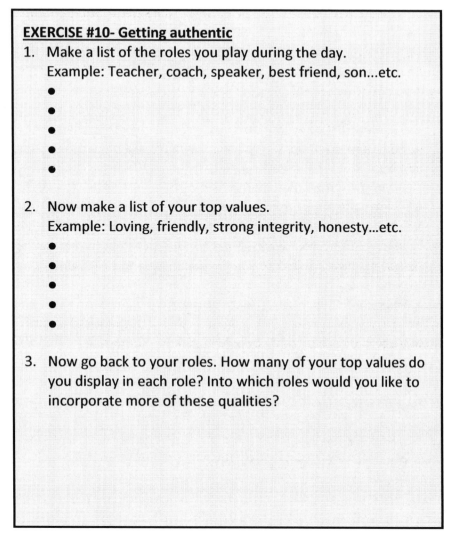

EXERCISE #10- Getting authentic
1. Make a list of the roles you play during the day.
   Example: Teacher, coach, speaker, best friend, son...etc.
   -
   -
   -
   -
   -

2. Now make a list of your top values.
   Example: Loving, friendly, strong integrity, honesty...etc.
   -
   -
   -
   -
   -

3. Now go back to your roles. How many of your top values do you display in each role? Into which roles would you like to incorporate more of these qualities?

PEOPLE-PLEASING

"Making others happy" can be a motivating factor for some goals. And if your motivation is to help other people, that can be good, right? Self-sacrifice is noble, right? Good people make sure their family, friends and co-workers are happy, right?

What about when helping other people means that you are sacrificing your own well-being? When this happens, we move from being "good people" to "people-pleasers". I am amazed at how often I see people dismiss their own feelings or desires in order to make other people happy.

What are some symptoms of people-pleasing?

- Regularly putting others' needs before your own
- Finding it hard to say "no"
- Getting upset because people seem to take advantage of you
- Regularly second guessing interactions. (Did I say the right thing? Are they mad at me?)
- Feeling guilty in interactions with others
- Finding yourself in one-sided conversations that don't allow you to talk about yourself (either due to the other person not asking how you are or your unwillingness to talk about yourself)
- Regularly making excuses for others

What do we get out of being people-pleasers? Some say they do it for the pure satisfaction of making another person happy. Though this may be true sometimes, more often than not, it is to obtain validation from others. It also can feel nice to be needed.

When I find myself people-pleasing, it usually comes from a feeling of unworthiness. When I feel unworthy or bad about myself, I have a tendency to search for others to validate me. If I can make them happy, then perhaps their gratitude or acknowledgement of my excellence will convince me I am worthy. Unfortunately, this fails because, if I don't believe I am worthy, then there is nothing anyone else can do to change my belief. Expecting others to constantly validate us is setting up an unrealistic expectation of them.

Some also use people-pleasing as an opportunity to avoid facing their own goals and dealing with their fear of failure. They say, "I wish I had more time to work on my project but my friend needs me to help him." They kill two birds with one stone. They look good for being of service and they don't have to work on their own stuff. In other words, they can't fail if they never try.

Believe it or not, people-pleasing can be very difficult to abandon. Society promotes it, friends can benefit from it and sometimes we get that momentary boost of self-esteem from others' validation. When we start letting go of our people-pleasing traits, it can be quite a shock to people in our life. At first, their disappointment can seem extreme, perhaps causing us more stress than the original people-pleasing. If we can make it through this, though, things do tend to balance out. Friends begin to accept our new way of being and some even start admiring us for taking care of ourselves. True friends want us to take care of ourselves.

If you find yourself people-pleasing:

- Practice saying "no" - even if someone may be upset or hurt
- Remind yourself that it is sometimes ok for others to be unhappy or disappointed without needing to fix it
- Give yourself permission to voice your opinions and desires
- Ask yourself what you really want
- Regularly take time for yourself, doing only what you want to do

By consciously trying to change this habit, our thinking slowly evolves from, "Everyone is more important than I am," to, "I am just as important as everyone else." And these habits build our self-esteem by validating our worthiness instead of depending on others to do it for us. When we have self-esteem, we validate our authentic selves. It's at this moment that we can begin to allow the life of dreams to manifest.

EXERCISE #11- Just say "no"

Rate on a scale from 1-10, how easy it is for you to say no to the following people:

1- Very hard/10- Very easy

Person	Rating	Fear of what might happen if you say no
Person you are dating/spouse		
Boss		
Mother		
Father		
Siblings		
Friends		
Acquaintances		
Co-workers		

VALUES

Creating the life of our dreams is, in short, putting into action our most important values. When these values are acknowledged and inspire our actions, we feel fulfilled. Many people think they know their values, but oftentimes they really don't. In fact, very few people can identify their deepest, most important values.

And fewer, still, are living those values.

I call it the sandpaper effect. It is the feeling that something isn't right - whether it's in making a decision or in a relationship - and it's almost like sandpaper being rubbed on an exposed nerve. When clients mention a feeling of uneasiness, irritability, restlessness or general discomfort, that's my cue as a coach to inquire about the validity of the values they are living.

Values are those principles or standards that determine for us what is important. As we progress in life, sometimes we forget what we value. For very innocent reasons, ranging from not wanting to upset people to not taking the time to assess what our true values are in a particular situation, we can slowly start making decisions that don't reflect our values. If we keep doing this, forgoing our values, we lose ourselves. Living life by our values is like using a muscle in the body. If we stop doing it, we grow weak.

Two things can be helpful in determining how well you are living your values. First, you must acknowledge them. Second, and perhaps more importantly, ask yourself which of those values you spend most of your energy on.

So what *do* you value? If you have never asked yourself this question, I highly suggest it. In fact, this is my first question with almost every new client. Most people have some general idea of the big things they value: Life, security, happiness, etc. But what about when values seem to conflict? Do you value being of service to others or making money? Silence or connecting to others? Honesty or friendship?

The next inquiry is into how well your actions are reflecting your values. If you value family but are away from them most of the year traveling for work, you might feel that sandpaper effect. If spiritual growth is a high value for you, but you are spending most of your day running around, unable to be quiet or connect to yourself, you might find yourself irritated, frustrated or just plain grumpy. If traveling to new places and discovering new cultures is of high value to you and you have three trips planned this year to different parts of the world, you might feel excited and exhilarated.

People can live years without realizing or acknowledging the sandpaper effect, the discomfort this produces. It becomes normal. Once acknowledged, though, it is hard to deny. Many times, simple acknowledgment of an action discordant with our values - and the discomfort that it brings - moves people to solve their internal conflict.

EXERCISE #12- Values*

Adapted from iPEC Coaching's "Values Assessment" exercise

-On the following page, circle those values that mean the most to you.

-Put a "+" next to those values that most influence your daily choices. (Note: some of these may not be values you circled and, thus, you end up feeling the sandpaper effect)

-Put an "x" next to those you want to be more conscious of when you make decisions. In other words, those values that you want to incorporate more fully into your life.

adventure	family	patience
autonomy	financial growth	persistence
beauty	flexibility	perspective
candor	freedom	power
challenge	friendship	productivity
clarity	fulfillment	profitability
cleverness	fun	prosperity
collaboration	growth	purposefulness
commitment	happiness	quality
communication	hard work	recognition
community support	harmony	relationships
competence	health	resources
competition	honesty	respect
control	honor	risk-taking
cooperation	hope	security
courage	humor	self-control
creativity	independence	service
curiosity	influence	simplicity
decisiveness	initiative	sincerity
dependability	innovation	spirituality
discipline	integrity	stewardship
diversity	intelligence	strength
effectiveness	justice	success
efficiency	learning	support
empathy	love	teamwork
environment	loyalty	truth
equality	obedience	trust
excellence	open-mindedness	variety
excitement	originality	wisdom

PAIN VS. GAIN

A great motivator for many clients is pain. The more pain a client feels about his life, the more willing he is, usually, to work to relieve that pain. A lot of people are mildly uncomfortable; they aren't exactly happy but nothing is seriously wrong in their lives. Being just mildly uncomfortable can be the biggest enemy in creating the life of your dreams.

When we are comfortable, why should we change? Imagine you are on the couch, all settled in, watching a great show on TV. Now the thought crosses your mind you would like a cookie. Immediately, you start to weigh leaving the comfort of the couch to get a cookie. If your comfort level is an 8 out of 10 and your desire for a cookie is a 4 out of 10, the couch will win. The need for the cookie is not causing enough discomfort for you to reject the comfort of the couch.

Now imagine you have been without food for 8 hours. The situation is a little different. You have the "pain" of being hungry. And your hunger is affecting your comfort on the couch. So your comfort level is a 4 out of 10 and your hunger is an 8 out of 10. Do you stay on the couch or do you get a cookie? You would choose the cookie this time. By choosing the cookie, you will relieve the pain of hunger and, thus, restore your comfort.

When I was a junior in college I took a mythology class. My initial thought was this probably wouldn't be the easiest class but I really wouldn't have to work that hard. I took the first test and felt like I would probably get a B on it.

I was wrong. I flunked the test. In fact my "F" was so low, there was no way, point-wise, I could get an "A" in the class. To say I was shocked was an understatement. Bob Kiser did not get "F's."

When I realized there was a good possibility that I could fail this class, I was mortified. In that moment I made the decision that was *not* going to happen.

All that semester I studied nonstop. It felt like every waking moment I was going over who Zeus was, who his son was, who he had made mad, etc. I learned each story from both the Greek perspective and the Roman. I was not going to fail this class.

I aced each test from that point on *plus* received all the bonus points. At the end of the semester, the professor called me over. He said technically I should not be getting an "A" but I had accomplished a first in this class. Since the initial exam, I had not missed any points. No one had ever gotten a perfect score on any of his exams, let alone three of them.

Now, it's important to say at this point, I was not a straight "A" student. I was happy with middle of the road grades. But this class proved to me (and my parents) that when I put my mind to it, when I made the decision, I was capable of great educational feats.

When the pain of possibly flunking this class presented itself, I got to work. And did the impossible- I got that "A" in Mythology.

In examining the "why" of your goals, I suggest looking at the pains and gains in relation to your intended goal. The more you can accentuate the pains you will be relieving, the more likely the goal will be achieved.

Looking at pain is especially helpful when you're trying to let go of old habits and create new ones.

In my own life, I got to this point with my finances. For awhile, I had been taking trips, feeling that the "gain" or pleasure of taking a trip outweighed the debt I might be accruing. My rationale was "you only live once!" I mean, come on. Saving money wasn't fun. The excitement of traveling was. This mindset worked until one specific trip

On an impromptu trip to Guam, I was unusually cranky. I was very concerned with money. Every expenditure brought more irritation. In a conversation with my travel companion, I finally realized I had hit my tipping point. The pain of accruing debt was now outweighing the joy of impromptu traveling.

After that point, staying home didn't feel like a sacrifice but rather a gift I was giving myself. My happiness was found each month in paying off my credit cards. I was willing to wait and save for my vacation with the anticipation that I would enjoy the trip that much more since the stress of finances wouldn't be there.

Another example:

I want to stop shopping so much.

	Pain	Gain
Shopping	• *Debt* • *Stuff I don't need* • *Wasting time* • *Husband upset* • *Hiding things* • *Feel guilty/remorseful*	• *Feel a rush/get excited* • *Love finding a sale* • *Get nice stuff* • *A lot of people like my clothes* • *Something to talk about* • *Something my friends and I love doing together*
Quit Shopping	• *Won't have the newest items* • *Will feel 'less than' other people* • *Miss spending time with friends since we won't be shopping.*	• *I would have more money* • *More time for my work & relationships* • *Husband won't be upset* • *Won't feel guilty or have to hide things*

The illustration above highlights the pains and gains of shopping too much. By seeing them written out, you may find that your values are not always what they seem. Shopping was a habit that left you feeling guilty, but it created a connection to friends (highlighted). It looks like you might want to lessen your shopping while finding something new to do with friends. New activities with friends might be the real driving value, the real gain that allows you to stop spending so much time shopping.

The ultimate goal we all seek is comfort. Sometimes people consider change but abort that goal because they fear it will bring discomfort or even chaos into their lives. If the perceived pain of change is greater than the perceived gain then usually we won't make the change. This is true even if our old habits are causing us great harm.

Joe came to see me because his life was in chaos and he was about to lose his wife. He was a police officer who recently had been hurt in the line of duty. He also was dealing with severe anxiety due to the many dangers he faced on the streets. That anxiety had given rise to uncontrolled anger and depression, which had greatly impacted his home life. His wife was fed up. She said either he had to quit the job or she was leaving. He even told me, initially, that he wanted to quit the force.

"Pretty straight forward," I thought. "This should be easy."

I was wrong. Deep down, Joe wasn't ready to stop being a police officer. On the surface, he could acknowledge the dangers his current position held. The job was costing him his health, marriage and even his sanity. And yet, something was not letting him move on.

During one session, he became very frustrated with me and said he was just going to turn in his resignation and be done with it. On the surface, if he had just quit, it would have been a successful coaching session. After all, one of his ultimate goals was to leave his job. But my gut told me he really didn't want to quit. At least not yet. If he quit now, he would be filled with regret. Since he was on leave for 6 months due to injury, I suggested that he wait. My hope was that he would get to a place where he wanted to quit instead of feeling like he was being forced.

After further exploration, we made a discovery. He didn't want to quit because of loyalty. He told me that even though he hated the job, his fellow officers were like his family. He had a duty to them. There is an unspoken agreement among police officers that they stand together. They witness extreme situations no one else could ever understand. Out of an "all for one" sense of survival, it is understood that your brothers always have your back.

To Joe, quitting meant he was turning his back on his brothers.

But he was also strongly devoted to his family at home, so we explored how his job affected them. I said I understood that he didn't want to abandon his police family but as a police officer, he was abandoning his family at home. The "ah-ha moments" started happening.

About a week later, he began the session by telling me he was getting excited about his future professional endeavors. Then, out of the blue he said:

"Oh, I forgot. I went to the station and turned in my resignation. Anyway, so I was thinking that…"

I stopped him. I was surprised. In the past weeks, quitting had brought him such anxiety. I was curious why the change.

He told me, "Yeah, all of a sudden it wasn't a big deal anymore. I just did it. Funny, I don't know why I was so reluctant. Anyway, I can't wait to tell you about…"

Luckily, we had taken the time to explore what he really, deep down, wanted. If Joe had begrudgingly quit, most likely he would have run into obstacles down *the road. He might have been forever wondering what could have been, forever focused on his regrets. And he probably would have resented his wife for making him quit his job.*

The desire to quit came from his authentic self. Joe took the time to acknowledge his feelings and values. He explored his actions and saw that they weren't congruent with his family's well-being, his top value. In fact, he had forgotten that the reason he had become a police officer was to provide for his family. When he realized that the job that once was helping his family was now destroying it, he was able to let it go.

CHAPTER 4 – GETTING INTO ACTION

Lisa, a brilliant comedian, writer and director, hired me to help improve her work efficiency. She had a problem focusing, at least that's what she thought. She seemed to be able to start things but rarely finish them.

After meeting with her, I realized Lisa did have the ability to follow through with goals as long as they were manageable. If a goal was too big, though, she would soon become overwhelmed, shut down and move on to the next goal without completing the first one.

We figured out what seemed to work for Lisa was chunking down her large goals into smaller, doable goals. And soon, by completing those smaller goals, she found she had finished the bigger goals she thought were too big for her.

Now, when she was overwhelmed, she had a tool to help her move forward.

Congratulations! By now you have a clear, precise vision of what you want. You also have a clear understanding of what your values are, and how they connect to making your dreams come true.

So let's get to work creating an action plan! There are some simple guidelines that go into effective goals. When followed, many potential obstacles can be avoided.

S.M.A.R.T. GOALS

In a 1981 paper entitled *"There's a S.M.A.R.T. way to write management goals and objectives,"* George T. Doran introduced a new way to create goals. His basic idea was that goals were more likely to be completed if they are:

S- *Specific*
M- *Measurable*
A- *Achievable*
R- *Realistic*
T- *Time-specific*

The brain loves to solve problems. The key, though, is in the specificity. If the goal is clear and seems doable, we usually won't have a problem completing it, provided, of course, that it is tied to our values. However, the brain has a tendency to shut down when we don't really understand what we are looking for and feel overwhelmed.

Specificity is the first trait of S.M.A.R.T. goals. With more general action plans, there is a tendency to wonder if enough has been accomplished. Should I do more? Maybe I should do this instead? Precious time can be spent on the continual discernment of what the goal really is rather than on completing the goal itself.

Let's take Linda, for example. She wants to change jobs. When asked about her goal for the upcoming week, she says that she will research possible opportunities on the Internet.

But what are Linda's more ***specific*** goals? Questions for Linda are:

- What kind of jobs are you looking for?
- What are the parameters?
- Where on the Internet will you be looking? Are you doing a Google search? Checking LinkedIn for job postings?

The **SPECIFIC GOAL** might be:

- To find job opportunities teaching in private schools, grades 4-6.
- Online, she will look at k12jobspot.com

Next, we need to know if the goal is **_measurable_**. Right now, very generally, Linda is just looking for some job opportunities.

Questions for Linda:

- How many listings will you examine on the site?
- What specific questions do you want answered from your research?

The **MEASURABLE GOAL** might be:

- She will look at *all* the job opportunities on the site.
- She will answer these questions:
    o Do I wish to work in that particular school district?
    o Is the job a 4-6th grade position?
    o Is it a temporary or permanent position?
    o What special requirements are required, if any, for this position? (special certifications, etc.)

Now the brain knows exactly what needs to happen for her research to be considered complete. The goal is specific and it is measurable. Her goal is now so specific and non-ambiguous that she will be more likely to accomplish it.

But how **_achievable_** is it to look at all the job possibilities on the site? If the mind feels the task is too big, it will get overwhelmed. The result can be procrastination and stress. When we can't motivate ourselves, we beat ourselves up.

There are at least 50 or more relevant job opportunities on the website Linda will be researching. Researching 50 seems like a lot and not very achievable.

Question for Linda:

- How many of these can a person be expected to research in a week?

The **ACHIEVABLE GOAL** might be:

- Research 20 schools

Under normal circumstances, 20 sites would be achievable. Then the question becomes whether Linda will have a normal week.

What might be achievable under the best of circumstances might not be possible at the present moment for any number of reasons. It's important to figure out if that goal is also ***realistic***.

This coming week, she is presenting at a conference and her daughter's recital is on Saturday. Twenty schools might not be doable for her.

So, she should set a more **REALISTIC GOAL** such as:

- Research 10 schools, answering the specific questions she came up with earlier.

Now, when is all this due? If they have a nebulous deadline, most people find it difficult to get the goal done. But if we know that a report is due on Friday, it is on our radar and motivates us to move forward. The more ***time-specific*** we can be with a deadline, the more effective our efforts will be.

Linda's current deadline is next week. A more **TIME-SPECIFIC GOAL** might be:

- At 5:00 p.m. on Tuesday, Linda will send me an e-mail verifying that she has accomplished this goal.

To be more effective, let's change that 5:00 p.m. to 4:53 p.m. Why? Our brains tend to consider times on the hour or half past as meaning "around" that time. When you say you will meet someone at 7:00 for dinner are you exactly on time? The ":53" is an unexpected time for the completion of the goal, cementing the challenge into our brains.

This idea comes from the personal experience of William Maddox, retired marketing director of Timken Company in Canton, Ohio. He says if you want a meeting to start on time, begin a little before the hour or a few minutes after. On the hour, some people will straggle in. Off the hour, people tend to show up on time.

To sum up: Linda's initial goal was to "research possible opportunities on the Internet."

Her new SMART goal: She will research job opportunities on k12jobspot.com and answer the following questions about 10 of them:

- Is the school in a district I want to work in?
- Is the job a 4-6th grade position?
- Is it a temporary or permanent position?
- What special requirements are there for this position?

She will email me at or before 4:53 p.m. on Tuesday to tell me she has completed her goal.

TO DO OR NOT TO DO (The benefits of the "To-Do" List)

If creating our dreams was as easy as creating that one perfect SMART goal then life would be, well, a dream. Usually, though, it takes multiple goals. And that's where issues can arise.

Ever feel overwhelmed with everything you have to do? Do you sometimes forget to do things? Not sure how to prioritize your time? Congratulations! You are pretty normal. In fact, these are some of the top reasons clients seek my assistance.

My suggestion: The ever-reliable "To-Do" list. Write down the things you need to do.

People are often overwhelmed with trying to remember everything they have to do. Just by simply setting it to paper, the mind can stop working so hard to remember it all. And once it is written, many people find they have less to do than they thought.

All some people need to move them into action is to write down their goals. They need not worry about the order, size or even how much they want the goal. It's about getting all the steps down. Others need a little organization in their list.

So they arrange them according to deadlines. This can help to prioritize time and balance workloads. Do you find everything is due on Friday? How about moving up one of those due dates to Wednesday? Can you push back one of those dates to Monday? Relieving the mental stress by making the list with deadlines can shift your focus from just remembering tasks to creating quality-driven results.

A second option is writing your lists by priority. These can range from high priority lists, meaning items that need to be done in the next 24 hours, to long term deadlines for things that, say, need to be done in the next 3 months. Listing by priority helps us use our time wisely to knock out important items, first.

For general to-do lists, here is a format I often use:

Check when done	Task	Materials needed to complete task	Due Date

I often suggest two things to think about in regards to a to-do list:

1. Make it at the end of the workday or right before you go to bed. That way you can start the following day with an already

prepared list. Most likely you will waste less time and will find it easier to remember where you left off the day before.

2. It's also handy in those moments of inspiration when you don't want to forget your thought! The goal is to lessen the need to remember things. Write them down as soon as you remember them. Then, when it is convenient, move those items to your "To-Do" list. Some clients keep paper with them in their coats, in the car, near their bed or even next to the shower (the shower is where I seem to get most of my ideas). This is especially helpful when you wake up in the middle of the night, having forgotten that important thing. Once on paper, it's easier to go back to sleep and more likely to get done the next day.

Some additional helpful hints:

- Start your list with one thing you have already done. Being able to mark that thing off your list makes it easier to continue to the rest.
- Do it consistently. As Jean de La Fontaine said, "One of the secrets of getting more done is to make a to-do List every day, keep it visible, and use it as a guide to action as you go through the day."
- Though most people organize their lists by due dates, some divide them into other categories such as: *Needs Immediate Attention*, or *Urgent*, or *Normal Priority*, or *Things to Do in Slower Times.*
- When reviewing your list each day, be open to the possibility that some of the "Normal Priority" items may need to be moved up to the "Urgent" list if they have not been completed.
- If you find yourself procrastinating or stalling on one of the items, perhaps it needs to be broken into smaller, more doable tasks.

> Example: "Need to send mom a birthday present" might need to be broken down into...

1. Decide on present for mom.
2. Go to mall to buy present or order it online.
3. Go to post office to mail present.

TO-DO LIST FOR OPENING A LEMONADE STAND

Let's say I'm planning to build a lemonade stand. I would start with my general "To-Do" list. This is just a list of everything I can think of that goes into my project.

1. Make lemonade
2. Make a booth
3. Get cups for the lemonade
4. Market my stand

Next I would rearrange my list in an order that makes sense:
1. Make a booth
2. Market my stand
3. Get cups for the lemonade
4. Make lemonade

Then, because each goal is pretty big, I would need to chunk down my "To-Do" list into something like this.

1. Make a booth
   a. Get a table from garage
   b. Get a chair
2. Market my stand
   a. Make 3 signs
   b. Put 1 on either end of street
   c. Put one sign on stand
3. Get some lemonade
   a. Ask mom to make the lemonade
   b. Take lemonade to stand
4. Get cups for the lemonade
   a. Get from Kitchen
   b. Take the cups to the stand

Then I would start on my chunked-down list. Because obstacles will probably come up, you may need to change your to-do-list.

Also notice in the following chart how "Go to store to buy cups" is connected to "Go to store to buy lemons." Parts of one action can help with the completion of another. To complete both, you have to go to the store. By thinking ahead and making a store "to-do" list, you can save time.

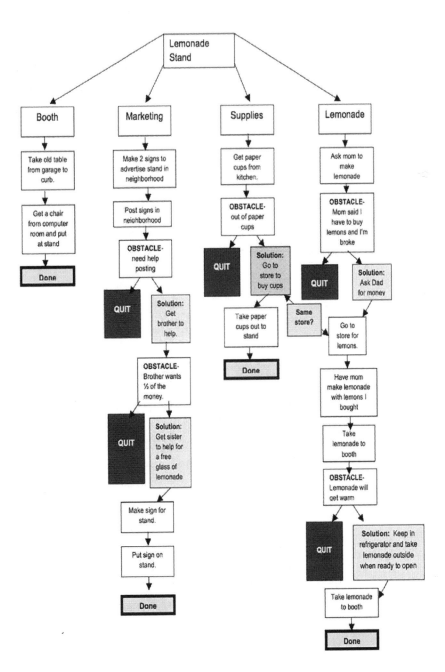

Lemonade Stand

Booth
- Take old table from garage to curb.
- Get a chair from computer room and put at stand
- **Done**

Marketing
- Make 2 signs to advertise stand in neighborhood
- Post signs in neighborhood
- OBSTACLE- need help posting
  - QUIT
  - Solution: Get brother to help.
- OBSTACLE- Brother wants ½ of the money.
  - QUIT
  - Solution: Get sister to help for a free glass of lemonade
- Make sign for stand.
- Put sign on stand.
- **Done**

Supplies
- Get paper cups from kitchen.
- OBSTACLE- out of paper cups
  - QUIT
  - Solution: Go to store to buy cups
    - Same store?
- Take paper cups out to stand
- **Done**

Lemonade
- Ask mom to make lemonade
- OBSTACLE- Mom said I have to buy lemons and I'm broke
  - QUIT
  - Solution: Ask Dad for money
- Go to store for lemons.
- Have mom make lemonade with lemons I bought
- Take lemonade to booth
- OBSTACLE- Lemonade will get warm
  - QUIT
  - Solution: Keep in refrigerator and take lemonade outside when ready to open
- Take lemonade to booth
- **Done**

HIRE IT OUT

Sometimes there are things on your list that need to get accomplished but just aren't happening for whatever reason. There is no shame in asking for help. Though free help is great, don't automatically dismiss the idea of paying someone. When you lack the interest or skills to accomplish a goal, the most effective choice may be to hire it out.

The question that usually determines if a client should hire something out is:

"How might your lack of experience, knowledge and/or interest actually hurt your end goal if you do it yourself?"

For example, much planning goes into creating a marketable website. It can be one of the most intimidating tasks for clients. Getting someone to build a website can be quite expensive. When starting a new venture, expenses are always a consideration. So an option most clients want to discuss is doing it themselves.

Do-it-yourself website builders are all over the Internet. But it's not just about building the site itself, but getting the search engines to pick up the website. It's also about making sure the content is well organized and easily searchable. So, yes, my client may save money on construction but ultimately lose even more money because people didn't see it or couldn't navigate it easily.

Other questions I have clients consider are:

- *How much time will it take you to do a task you have very little knowledge about and even less talent for?*
- *Will devoting time to this step take you away from the things you really should be doing?*
- *How vital is it to the goal that you, personally, do this action step yourself?*

GOING AROUND VS. GOING THROUGH AN OBSTACLE

When it comes to goals, almost everyone encounters obstacles. Unsuccessful people tend to be those who: 1) give up when confronted with an obstacle or 2) deny that the obstacle exists and end up being defeated by that "non-existent" obstacle. An example of the latter would be the freshman who thinks she doesn't need to study.

Successful people deal with the obstacles. They see them as challenges and opportunities. They can either go through obstacles or around them.

To go through an obstacle means we simply fix, or address it, head on. The game plan is usually to eliminate the obstacle. Take an architect who is hired to build a house. His obstacle is that there are trees in the middle of the chosen property. The most direct solution would be to simply cut down the trees and build the house.

When we go around an obstacle we look for a different route to the goal or, in some cases, an alternative goal. Changing the original goal in a way that the obstacle no longer exists is an example. Instead of cutting down the trees, the architect decides to build the house 500 feet away from them. True, the house is not exactly where originally planned, but it's close enough and it saves the trees.

Another way to go around an obstacle is to incorporate it into the goal. To do this, our architect might, literally, design the rooms around the tree. He could design comfortable rooms with the trees in the middle of them. Or another alternative is he might design a tree house up in the trees!

Sometimes it's about looking more closely at our obstacles to make sure they are truly obstacles.

Sir Alexander Fleming, a scientist, was trying to come up with a cure for diseases. He thought he had failed. Then he noticed one of his discarded petri dishes contained a mold dissolving the bacteria around it. He had accidentally discovered penicillin.

A cook named George Clum was cooking a plate of fried potatoes. After a customer kept sending back his potatoes to be fried even longer, Clum got so mad he decided to cut the potatoes really thin and fry them an extraordinary long time. Unexpectedly, the customer loved them and ordered more. George Clum had invented the potato chip.

I try to encourage my clients to get excited about challenges instead of dreading them. Why? First of all, they are inevitable. If you want to succeed, you will have to deal with obstacles—so you might as well get a good attitude about them. It's just more pleasant.

But also, sometimes those obstacles we most dread will lead to our greatest successes. Many obstacles in my life have made me a better person. In many cases, I acquired new skills to get through the obstacles. Other times, I gained new faith in myself. Skills and faith— both are very powerful things. I'm pretty sure, if you look deep down, the same has happened or will happen to you.

HELP! I NEED SOMEBODY

In creating the life of your dreams, you have to be comfortable asking for help. I have rarely seen bigger goals completed without assistance. We all need help from time to time.

But, the question often becomes, *Help from whom?* Too often I have seen clients break through their reluctance to ask for help only to sabotage themselves by asking the wrong people. It's about looking at the thing you need help with and finding the best person for the job. Adapted from Rhonda Britten's *Fearless Living Program,* here is one way to think of categorizing your support network:

- **Cheerleaders**: Usually your family and friends; these are the people who are always there, no matter what, reminding you that you can do it. Their support has little to do with

70

knowledge of your goal but with loyalty and love for you as a person.

- **Knowledgeable Comrades:** People who have more knowledge about your particular goal than your cheerleader buddies probably have. They may act as cheerleaders, but they also hold you accountable and give you their opinions. Fellow students and colleagues can fall into this category.
- **Sage Counsel:** These are people who have gone before you and are there to tell you what worked for them and what didn't. Though some cheerleading may occur, the knowledge these people supply is their way of supporting you. Consultants, coaches and mentors fall into this category.
- **Symbiotic Partnerships**: People that want to help you because you might be able to help them. They may or may not be in your field. An example is a massage therapist and wellness coach who refer clients to each other. All can gain from this arrangement. The massage therapist and coach get new clients and clients get specialized help from an additional practitioner.

My client, Carrie, was a fantastic actress. She had a habit, though, of looking for personal validation from professional mentors. One particular instance was with a well-known director. This director had made it very clear he was impressed with her talent. During rehearsals, though, Carrie felt that the director didn't like her. This had happened before with other shows and with other directors.

> "How do you know the director doesn't like you?" I asked.

> "During breaks, he doesn't talk to me. He talks to the dancers but will rarely even look at me. I've tried everything. I even brought him some cookies. He barely muttered a thank you."

> "What does he say about your performance?"

"He says I'm great. He laughs at my lines. He loves my voice. Yesterday, though, he seemed to get mad at me. I just had a question but he seemed really annoyed with me. Maybe I asked at the wrong time. After that, I felt like I didn't perform as well. He's probably starting to hate my performance now. I'm never going to work for him again."

"Carrie, I've got a question for you. Why are you doing this show?"

"It's a big profile project plus I really wanted to work with this director."

"Ok. Why do you want to work for this director?"

Hesitantly, Carrie said, "I want to learn from him. He's been in the business a long time. I also want him to see how good I am so he hires me again."

"Is that all?"

Carrie knew my tricks by now. She grinned at me. "I think so, but I have a feeling you are about to lay a bombshell on me."

I laughed. "Are you there to make friends or to work?"

She looked at me in silence. (This is how I know I have hit a button with a client.)

After a while she said very pointedly, "I'm there to work. I'm a professional. Oh, my God! I have been trying to get his approval as a friend."

"It sure sounds like it. From what you have told me, he thinks you're very talented and doing a great job *in the show. From what I know about you, I'm almost certain that is the truth. Unfortunately, though, it sounds like your desire to win him as a friend might be sabotaging your success in this show. What do you think?"*

"I think you are right! And to tell you the truth, he's worked with almost everyone in this show before. I'm the new kid. Wow! Okay, new plan. Do my job and enjoy it. If I make friends, so be it but not a necessity."

"Nice!"

Carrie should have considered the director part of her Sage Counsel. Instead, she tried to make him a knowledgeable comrade that also acted as a cheerleader, and thus, had unrealistic expectations of their relationship. Or in the words of an old saying: "Unrealistic expectations lead to pre-meditated resentments."

To conclude this story, when Carrie let go of her need to get the director to like her personally, they became good friends. In fact, as I was writing this, I noticed that she was starring in his forthcoming show.

SUMMARY

A lot goes into creating effective goals. Making "SMART" goals can provide the specificity needed for an achievable goal. Larger goals sometimes need to be broken down into smaller, more manageable chunks.

Multiple action steps can still overwhelm. That's when organization comes into play using our handy "to-do" lists. Effectively organizing your action plan can be the difference between a "shelved" project and a huge success.

And even with the best goals and organization, we usually need help. Remember that obtaining appropriate help is essential. Having unrealistic expectations about the kind of help your support network can provide may lead to resentments that sabotage your success.

Now that we have the essential ingredients for taking action, you should be able to create the life of your dreams, right?

Theoretically, yes. Realistically, no. We have more things to consider...

CHAPTER 5 – OBSTACLES: WHAT COULD GET IN YOUR WAY?

I asked students in my graduate seminar if they thought people could really do anything they wanted.

Josh told me, "No."

He went on to say, "I have heard this crap a lot but I think it's important for people to know their limitations. They have to be realistic. I mean if someone wants to be a professional dancer but they are in a wheelchair, they just won't be able to do it."

I thought. "He might have me here." (Yes, we coaches lose faith also!)

Just as I was about to address his comment, another student raised her hand:

"My sister was a professional dancer before a car accident that paralyzed her legs. She's in a wheelchair now and yet still dances professionally. She is part of a dance troupe that uses dancers in chairs. She also performed in a piece with a major dance company BECAUSE she was in a chair. She was exactly what they wanted."

"Well, you know what I mean..." Josh replied.

It was very cool that this student's sister continued her dream to dance. She probably had a "Josh voice" in her head, telling her she would never dance professionally again but if there was, she didn't listen to it.

Or rather, she didn't believe it.

Remember in Chapter 2 how I told you not to worry about thoughts of failure? We purposely ignored the possible obstacles in order to allow you to dream big. Well, the time has come to talk about those roadblocks that might get in the way of creating the life of your dreams.

I love the old saying "You can do anything you want if you set your mind to it." Most people love stories about people who have beaten the odds to have their dreams come true.

Probably most people, at one time or another, have had that voice inside that tells them, "But you can't do it." The difference between people who create the life of their dreams and those who don't is the former don't listen to it. Instead they tell it, "Watch me..."

EXERCISE #13: Making the decision to change

Sometimes all that is needed is acknowledgement of an obstacle and then making the decision to move past it. What can help is looking at how it is affecting your life.

Below is a simple exercise to help assess your willingness to move forward.

The problem is…	How would my life be different if you could change this thing?	What is stopping me?	On a scale from 1-10, how willing am I to change this thing? (1: not interested)	What is one step you are willing to take and when will you do it?
I don't have enough money to produce my movie	• Less stress • Could be artistically free • Wouldn't have to work 3 jobs	• Don't know where to get money • Nervous asking people for money	I want to really make movies so a 10	• Research funding options and have three possibilities by Friday

INTERNAL OBSTACLES VS. EXTERNAL OBSTACLES

All obstacles to our goals can be broken into two categories: external and internal. External obstacles are those things outside of us that create roadblocks in reaching our goals. An example might be when a couple plans to have their wedding in a garden and it rains. The rain is outside of the couple's control. In order to have the wedding, they will have to navigate around the rain, possibly by having it indoors.

A lot of people blame their inability to achieve their goals on what they say are external obstacles. Truth is, though, I rarely see outside obstacles that make it completely impossible for people to achieve their goals. Yes, outside obstacles can require an extra action step or two but usually they aren't the main reason coaching clients stumble.

Most of the time, it's their internal obstacles, the roadblocks they create themselves that keep them from succeeding. An example is the man who is financially well off but says, "I would try that if I had the money". Or the woman who really wants to go back to school but says she can't because her family needs her. The truth is both are probably scared they might fail and feel it's safer not to try at all.

FEAR

Fear is the root of almost all internal blocks. Time and time again, I see extremely talented individuals paralyzed by fear. And like quicksand, usually the harder they fight against it, the more they sink.

It is important to look at the validity of any particular fear. Is it real or imagined? Rational or irrational? The first step in addressing any fear is acknowledging its existence. Then with real fears, since they are based in reality, it's about making a game plan that addresses what you will do if the fears come to fruition.

Irrational fears are overblown with little or no chance of coming true. We can be sure the imaginary goblin under the bed will not attack the child. Why would anyone have irrational fears? It is a tool our subconscious has developed to keep us in our safety zone. If we fear something then we are less likely to take risks. Irrational fears hold people back more often than you might think. Great thing about these fears is that once their absurdity is acknowledged, they usually disappear.

My client, Steve, had just this type of fear so we examined it.

I asked him, *"Is that really true? Will you become homeless?"*

After thinking a bit, he realized this was probably not true:

"Truth is I have enough saved up to last a year if I lost my job. Worst-case scenario, my family would take me in. I could live with my sister if need be. I wouldn't be homeless...but just a second ago, it sure felt like I could be..."

His fear was VERY real to him even if the chance of becoming homeless was not. It is important to address all fears. To move beyond our fears, we need to explore the truth about the fear and figure out if it's rational or irrational. Then we need to make a game plan to address the fear and move past it.

Or we can just allow our fear to control us.

EXERCISE #14: Boo!

Here is an exercise to assess your fears.

I am afraid of...	How does this fear affect your life?	Is it a rational or irrational fear? Why?	What am I willing to do about this?
Spiders	I am always looking for spiders. I refuse to go into rooms unless someone goes with me. I'm afraid to sleep because I might get bitten in my sleep and die.	Irrational: an average of 6.6 people die each year from spider bites (Langley, R.L. *Animal-Related Fatalities in the United States - An Update Wilderness and Environmental Medicine* Vol. 16 pp. 67-74)	I am willing to think about the statistics next time I'm afraid.

WHEN YOU ASSUME...

It is impossible for us to know everything that is going on around us at any given second. There are so many stimuli the mind can't process them all. We NEVER know the whole truth. In fact this is why two people, in the same room at the same time, can have totally different perspectives on the same event.

Instead of just accepting our lack of information, our brains have a tendency to make up things. It fills in the missing information. Sometimes it's correct and sometimes it's not.

> *At 3:00 p.m. on Elsa's birthday, her boyfriend calls to say that he needs to delay their dinner. He would be*

running late. Elsa is surprised. She suddenly starts making a case against her boyfriend. Why is he going to be late? Doesn't he love her? Why would he do this? Is he seeing somebody else? She just knows he's probably cheating on her. AND he had the audacity to see the other woman on her birthday? She decides she needs to break-up.

When he finally arrives to pick her up, she is mad! Due to her interpretations of his actions, she gives him the silent treatment, letting him know that she feels mistreated.

When they get to the restaurant, the host escorts the couple towards a door in the back. Elsa's boyfriend opens it to a dark room. Confused, she walks in to suddenly hear "Surprise!" The lights come on to reveal all of her closest friends.

THEN Elsa sees her family from Mexico City. Her boyfriend had flown them all in to be with her. She learns that is why he was running later. Flights got delayed and he had to make other arrangements to get them to the restaurant.

Elsa was mortified at how she had treated her boyfriend...

The only information Elsa had was that her boyfriend would be running late. The rest of the "information" she made up. And like most of us, her mind made up a scary story. These thoughts really are meant to protect us. The thought is that if we can prepare ourselves for the worst, then it won't hurt or affect us as much. What's strange is that usually our worst fears NEVER happen!!!

Unfortunately, in this case, Elsa forgot that it was just an interpretation she had made up. She reacted to her belief by being nasty to her boyfriend. I wish I had a dollar for every time a client (or myself) reacted with a misinterpretation of a situation only to later regret it.

The problem is not that we make assumptions. It is that we usually don't take the time to investigate the validity of those assumptions. When creating the life of our dreams, fear will be present. Thus, it's good to be on the lookout for fear coloring our assumptions. Take time to ask yourself, "Is this true? How do I know that it's true?" Because our dreams are so personal, fear can make it hard to know when we believe an assumption. We tend to trust in anything our thoughts and emotions tell us.

Ask your friends to listen for any fearful assumptions you might be making when you are talking about your goals. Hopefully they can, lovingly, point out areas you might want to examine.

GREMLINS

Probably almost everyone has that voice inside that says they won't be able to do it. The "it" can be anything. This voice usually is a defensive mechanism we have developed around past failures (or perceived failures).

In coaching, we call this voice a Gremlin. We think of them as little monsters on our shoulders telling us we can't do something. They are based on our perceived notion of the truth.

Gremlins are hard to spot. After all, they are echoing beliefs we have about ourselves. The best way to spot a Gremlin is when we make "I" statements about our weaknesses.

> *"I can't sing"*
> *"I am a very bad public speaker"*
> *"I could never write a book because I'm horrible at writing"*

When working with our Gremlins, most of us get scared, upset or even mad. It is frustrating to think this "thing" is keeping us from succeeding. I have found, though, we have to make friends with our Gremlins in order for them to release their control on us. It's like the Chinese Finger Trap, the contraption that locks your fingers when you try to pull them out of it. The more you fight against the Gremlin, the more control it exerts over you. It's not about fighting the Gremlin but rather acknowledging and then negotiating.

The Gremlin is born out of an experience our subconscious doesn't want us to repeat. It believes it is protecting us. Its job: to make sure we never feel hurt or humiliated again. The bad part is that while gremlins are really good at their jobs they don't see the whole picture. They think they are helping us. Instead, they are usually hurting us by keeping us from our dreams.

Be aware that more Gremlins may come out as you get closer to creating the life of your dreams. When you start to feel like you just can't do something, pause. Check to see if maybe a Gremlin is voicing its concern.

I have a Gremlin. His name is Charlie. His job- to make sure I don't sing off pitch. See, when I was 10, I was given a part in a musical that had a lot of solos. I thought I sounded great. People had always been impressed with my voice.

Then a friend of mine told me I was singing flat.

I was shocked. Flat? What was flat? I had never even heard of this. Come to find out, I was singing below the pitches. I was mortified! Here I thought I was doing a great job and, from what I could gather, I had been making a fool out of myself!

From then on, it was always in the back of my head to not sing flat. When I was off pitch, I always felt that same mortified feeling as when I was 10. I went on to sing professionally but the nagging fear that I might be off pitch never left.

At one point the fear started to consume me. I started monitoring my singing, trying to sing softly to be as inconspicuous as possible. Confidence affects how much air a singer uses to make pitches. Due to my lack of confidence, I really did start going off pitch. My worst fears were coming true.

During a voice lesson, I just KNEW I was off pitch. My voice teacher kept saying I wasn't. I was very confused. Finally I decided my voice teacher must not be able to hear it or she was lying to me.

Then someone brought up the fact that my VERY professional, world renowned opera singing voice teacher probably could tell if someone was off pitch. They also pointed out that she probably wouldn't lie to me about it either.

At that moment, I realized it was me. I was getting in my own way. I had a voice inside my head telling me I couldn't sing on pitch. This was my first introduction to the idea of Gremlins.

Per my friend's suggestion, I decided to have a talk with my Gremlin. In my mind, I asked him why he was telling me I couldn't sing. The answer came to me. He was protecting me so I wouldn't make a fool of myself like I did when I was 10. Above all else, he was scared of my not knowing I was off pitch and someone telling me or, worse, laughing.

I first thought this Gremlin was against me but then realized he was on my side. Unfortunately, he didn't know that he was making things worse. He was making me hesitate, causing me not to be able to sing. I then told him I was not a 10-year old novice singer but rather a professional now who had a lot of experience. Plus I had a great teacher helping me.

I asked him what needed to happen so he would quit interfering with my singing.

The answer came quite quickly. He wanted me to be the first to know if I was off-pitch. I then remember my voice teacher recommending I record my auditions and performances and then listen to them. I asked Charlie if he thought that would help. Believe it or not, simply recording my singing and checking to make sure I was on pitch helped Charlie calm down. Yes, I still heard him in my head, but at least I could sing through it.

Getting past our Gremlins means we have to have a "chat" with them. The goal is to see what they are protecting us from. Then we need to bring them up to speed, to let them know their actions are actually hurting instead of helping us. Then we need to come to an agreement so they will allow us to move forward. Usually this entails coming up with a way for our Gremlins to protect without paralyzing us.

EXERCISE #15: Working with your Gremlin

What's your Gremlin's name?	
Imagine what it looks like, sitting on your shoulder. Draw a picture of it.	
What does it tell you?	
What's is its job? What is it trying to protect you from? When/why was it born?	
Thank the Gremlin for protecting you.	
How does this Gremlin affect you today? What does it keep you from doing?	
What does it need to know about you today? How are you different than the first time this happened? How are you qualified to protect yourself today without its help?	
What, if anything, needs to happen for the Gremlin to stop being an obstacle?	
If applicable, what is your action plan to move forward? Does your Gremlin agree? Does it need anything else?	

Thank your Gremlin for talking. Tell it you value its opinion and welcome its feedback. The only rule is that it can't stop you from living your dreams.

SELF-SABOTAGE (or The "Feel Good Meter")

A lot of my clients fear success. When I mention this to them, they usually laugh and reply: *"Why would anyone be scared of success?"* That's a great question! Why WOULD anyone be scared of success? One of the best books on the subject is *"The Big Leap"* by Gay Hendricks. He beautifully summarizes 4 beliefs people can have that cause them to sabotage their success:

1. **I can't have success because I am fundamentally flawed.**

2. **I would be disloyal to family and/or friends if I succeed.**

3. **I would be a burden to people in my life and/or success would be a burden to me.**

4. **I would outshine those around me if I succeed.**

Most people have a success thermostat inside themselves. This "Feel Good Meter" is set at a certain level. If we start getting what we deem too much success, our subconscious has a tendency to help us lower our success back down to our comfortable level. We self-sabotage.

We do this in a number of ways: procrastination (from which I suffered writing this book!), altercations, overspending, addictive behaviors and negativity – just to name a few. You don't need to look very far for examples. Look at any number of young superstars. Drug addiction, inappropriate videos, encounters with the law: all good ways to subdue success.

As for myself, I was comfortable being a big fish in a small pond. I was always looking to swim in the big ponds but they intimidated me. I was looking for the validation of the big fish but, secretly, thought I would never be good enough for them.

Due to my lack of confidence, I sabotaged more than one opportunity. How did I do this? I had lots of ammunition. Anything from being sick the day of a big event to starting a fight with the key people who gave me opportunities. Basically I was scared they were going to find out I was a fraud with no talent.

Here is the event that completely opened my eyes:

I was given the opportunity to direct a play at a great theater, but the invitation made me very nervous. In fact I had already declined an earlier invitation to direct for them, citing my schedule.

Throughout rehearsal, I was very careful to control my temper. I knew my tendency towards self-sabotage. On opening night I remember saying to my friend sitting next to me, "The show is going great! It shouldn't be going this well." BINGO! I had voiced my self-defeating thought.

During the second act, I noticed one of the actors seemingly break character and smile at friends in the audience. Then he flubbed a couple of lines. I was furious. The thought was, "He is ruining my show." (Notice the "MY" part of that last statement). After the show, the producer was exceptionally happy with the show, saying he wanted me to direct a forthcoming show. I mentioned my observation about the actor. The producer said I could talk to the actor but he didn't think it was a big deal. (Note that he saw something but it wasn't earth-shattering like I perceived it to be.)

I furiously cornered the actor. I lost it. Unfortunately the rest of the cast and crew witnessed my outburst. The rest of opening night had a cloud over it. The producer did not ask me back.

I had reacted out of a fear of success. My thought was "The show should not be going this well" and I searched out something to prove my point. Yes, the actor fell short, but due to my fear, I blew his minor shortcoming up into a bigger deal than it was.

So what is the solution? How do we let go of self-sabotaging?

1. When you notice the self-sabotage action and/or thought, simply stop and pause.

2. After some time has passed, go back and try to acknowledge, first, what your fearful thought was and, second, what success it was trying to prevent. (It could be as simple as you were feeling "too happy.")

3. Redo the situation in your mind. If you could do it all over again, what choices would you make? What different thoughts would you choose?

In my situation, I realized I have a tendency to exaggerate things when I am afraid. If I could redo the situation, I would have, casually and quietly, said to the actor, "Hey, I noticed you weren't as focused tonight as you were during rehearsals. Please stay in character even if you have friends in the audience." And then let it go.

To this day, when I find myself angry, I pause. Then I talk to another person for perspective. My goal is to never again treat another human being with disrespect or embarrass them.

EXERCISE #16: Release the brakes

Fill in the chart below.

Where in my life am I sabotaging my own success?	How does it affect my success?	Which of the following 4 self-sabotaging beliefs are causing me to create my obstacle(s)? (Circle the ones that are true)	Turn around your self-sabotaging belief and see how this might be as true or truer than your original thought	Am I willing to release this belief? What is one step I am willing to take to move forward?
EXAMPLE: Handling money	I stay in debt. When I do have extra money, I spend it quickly. I feel anxious with extra money. I make what families of 4 live on yet I am in debt.	• I can't have success because I am fundamentally flawed. • I would be disloyal to family and/or friends if I succeed. • I would be a burden to people in my life or success would be a burden to me. • I would outshine those around me if I succeed.	Even though my family doesn't have a lot of money, they would be happy for me if I became wealthy. I don't think more money has to overwhelm me or burden my life. It's about the handling of the money. When I do get overwhelmed I can ask for help instead of going into avoidance and spending recklessly.	Yes…I am going to talk to a financial planner on steps to let go of debt.
		• I can't have success because I am fundamentally flawed. • I would be disloyal to family and/or friends if I succeed. • I would be a burden to people in my life or success would be a burden to me. • I would outshine those around me if I succeed.		
		• I can't have success because I am fundamentally flawed. • I would be disloyal to family and/or friends if I succeed. • I would be a burden to people in my life or success would be a burden to me. • I would outshine those around me if I succeed.		

FEAR BUSTING

When you get stuck with your fears, some of these "solutions" may help:

Acknowledge your exact fear. Either write or say something like "I am afraid of 'X'." If 'X' happened, then I am afraid it would affect me in the following ways..." It is important to be as specific as possible. During this process, there is a possibility you may judge yourself for your fear. Try to let go of these judgments. If you are afraid of the dark, you are afraid of the dark.

Truth is an enemy of fear. It's time to question the validity of your fear. Is this a rational or irrational fear? Let's look at the fear of flying. The logical part is that most commercial planes fly about 35,000 feet off the ground. If the plane malfunctions and you fall from that height you will most likely die. But when you research it, the chances of being killed in a single airline flight, based on 78 major airlines, are 1 in 11 million. To put this in perspective, your chances of being killed in a car accident in one year are 1 in 5,000. So, as Harold Mass points out, "You're much more likely to die getting to the airport than you are flying in the planes." (The Week, July 8, 2013)

Look at how this fear affects your life. Something to keep in mind is fear can serve both positive and negative functions. First, write down the ways your fear keeps you safe (e.g., being afraid of tornadoes causes you to be super aware of tornado watches, and thus, more likely to seek safety). Next write down how your fear is creating obstacles in your life. What does it keep you from doing that you really want to be doing? What does it cause you to do that you otherwise wouldn't be doing? (Like a hypochondriac wasting money by repeatedly going to the doctor.) Also note how it affects the people around you.

Finish these statements

- My fear keeps me from
doing_____,
something I really want to do.
- My fear causes me to do

_____,
something I don't want to do.
- My fear affects other people in the following
ways:

_____

_____

_____

_____

After you have examined your fear, it is time to choose whether you will keep it or because of its harmful effects on your life, let it go. If you choose to let it go, I suggest turning that choice into a physical action. Write the fear on a piece of paper. Fold the paper and hold it in your hands, affirming to the powers that be in the universe that you are releasing the fear and asking for help in doing so. Lastly, burn the paper or tear it up and throw it away.

People tend to avoid things they fear. Unfortunately, this can reinforce the fear. Another choice is to try taking small steps toward the thing you fear. It's like dipping your toe in the pool to see how cold it is. The goal is to re-write the story of that fear by acknowledging *any* small successes. If the thing you feared does happen, note how you are affected.

Let's say I am afraid of speaking to groups of people because I fear that I will forget what to say. It feels like if this happened, I would die of embarrassment. It so happens that at one event I do forget some small part of my speech. At first I am upset. Then I stop and process the experience. How did this experience, truly, affect me? I did feel embarrassed but I didn't die or suffer other terrible consequences. When I talk to people afterward, I learn they hadn't even noticed my memory lapse or they had forgotten about it. And actually one person said if I had not called attention to it, he wouldn't have noticed it. What did I learn from processing this experience? It's not such a big deal if I do happen to forget something when speaking to a group.

PERFECTIONISM

Perfectionism can be another manifestation of fear and it presents an interesting dilemma for coaches. Perfectionists' commitment to achieving the highest quality can be astonishing. And as a coach, I definitely want my clients to strive to be their very best.

Unfortunately, though, there are pitfalls to perfectionism. Yes, these individuals sometimes achieve more than others, but their focus on the perfection of the outcome often impedes their enjoyment of the process. This intense focus usually means they base much of their self-worth on the results of their work. If they feel they have failed at a project, then they feel they have failed as human beings.

Some perfectionists focus so much on doing everything perfectly they find it hard to meet deadlines. They get bogged down in the details. They simply can't move on until the part they are working on is perfect.

Relationships with perfectionists can be difficult due to their unrealistically high expectations of themselves (and others). Basically, perfectionists need to feel like they are in control and they do this by trying to make sure everything is "right."

Perfectionism is something I have had to really examine in my own life. I thought that I should have very high standards. Striving to be perfect was noble. It meant that I was *really* trying. And by an intense effort, it would be possible to be good at everything and that I would finally feel ok.

Notice I did not say great or even good.

Unfortunately, my perfectionism led me to despair and depression. One big example was my inability to accept compliments. It got so bad I literally thought that people were lying to me, almost making fun of me, if they gave me a compliment. Nothing I achieved was good enough for me. If it wasn't good enough for me, then how could it be good enough for them?

I had to be great at everything I attempted. If I thought I couldn't do it well, I didn't do it. I hated to let anyone see me fail.

Not a fun way to live. Can you relate?

Luckily there are things that you can do to start relieving yourself of the perfectionist albatross:

- **Examine your perfectionism:** Ask yourself, "If I was not perfect, what am I afraid would happen? What would that mean about me?" Getting to such core beliefs can help a lot. For me, it was the fear that if I did not succeed, I would be abandoned. I would be rejected and, ultimately, alone. I discovered that actually it was easier for people to be around me when I wasn't trying to be "perfect Bob." My perfectionism pushed people away because I was so uptight all the time.
- **Be okay with imperfections:** This is a big one. It's important to accept your imperfections and hopefully, at some point, begin to love them. This doesn't mean you aren't going to keep trying to be better. It means you will be kind to yourself in the process. So how about planning one thing a week you know you aren't good at but enjoy doing? To bump this up a notch, plan the activity with friends, people who will support you in not being perfect. The goal is to enjoy the activity, not to succeed at it.
- **Search for humor:** One of the greatest gifts a friend gave me was laughing at me. I was upset because something wasn't going the way I had planned. He started laughing. I was angry

because I believed he was making fun of me. He just kept laughing. Finally I started laughing and in that moment, that pivotal moment, all my anxiety and stress melted away. I could see I was being unreasonable by being too hard on myself. After that I was able to go back to the task with a clear head. Next time you are stressed over a minor detail, try to find some humor.

- **6-month perspective:** When I start to get stressed about something, I ask myself, "Will this really matter in 6 months? Will I even remember this in 6 months?" If the answer is no, then I know I need to lighten up.

Ultimately, the reason to address one's perfectionism is because it harms quality of life. Perfectionists are rarely at peace. They have too much to worry about. Imagine a life where you could work hard *and* be happy. It's in accepting our imperfections that we find perfection.

PROCRASTINATION/LAZINESS

Laziness is a term I hear thrown around a lot. When people aren't doing what they think they are supposed to, they have a tendency to label themselves as lazy. Having been a coach for a while now, I have to say I rarely find people are lazy. When people are invested in a goal, knowing they will be getting something out of its completion, it usually gets done. When people dub themselves lazy it is usually because of being overwhelmed, confused about the purpose of their goal or plain not wanting to achieve it.

Laziness may be the symptom for different types of issues:

Issue: Overwhelmed

If you are saying things like, "Where do I start? I can't possibly do all this." or you feel like you are just shutting down mentally and stalling then you are overwhelmed. Many times, people procrastinate due to being overwhelmed. A goal that seems daunting, almost too big, can feel like it causes the brain to short-circuit and, thus, shut down.

Solution: Break it down
Break down those larger goals into smaller, doable amounts. From these, create a to-do-list with each smaller goal getting its own due date and plan of action.
Example: I need to get Cole (Kari's son) a savings bond.

Broken down:

1. Get information on where to get a savings bond.
2. Call the establishments and find out what is involved.
3. Decide where to buy the bond.
4. Go to that establishment and buy the savings bond.

NOTE: For you perfectionists who become overwhelmed due to trying to find the best answer, the key is to come to an acceptance that it might not be perfect. Promise yourself you will go on to the next step when the previous one is completed *even* if it is not perfect. Something to weigh is the time wasted spent trying to be perfect versus spending that time working on another task.

Issue: "I get stressed out waiting till the last minute but that's just how I work."
Some clients love the adrenaline rush they receive by waiting till the last minute. Like a drug, they crave the excitement it can produce. They can also crave the danger-like feeling. Will they get it done?

Others who wait till the last minute believe (subconsciously) they are fundamentally flawed and, if they procrastinate, then people won't make this discovery. Waiting till the last minute and having a goal or task be unsuccessful, they can blame it on not having enough time. But if they make sure they have plenty of time and *still* fail, then the spotlight would be on their abilities. True, some people may judge them for procrastinating but that is easier to take than people finding out their ultimate secret.

Solution: Acknowledge it, then accept or change it.

First, acknowledge your procrastination and, more importantly, how it truly affects your life. Perhaps you just need to accept that this is how you work. You actually like the feelings that procrastination produces. Simply by acknowledging that this is how you work, a lot of the stress may disappear.

But if you do find this is a habit you want to change, you need to dig a little deeper. Get to the truth of why you wait and how it is truly affecting you. Then I suggest, little by little, moving up your start time. If a project is due on Friday and you plan to start Thursday night at 6:00 p.m., perhaps start at 5:00 p.m. instead. Then gradually keep moving back start times. Take note if you feel more stress or less stress. Lastly, as you are trying to adopt a new way of working, be gentle with yourself. You will undoubtedly slip and go back to your old, familiar habit of procrastinating every once in awhile. Just try your new habit again next time.

Issue: I don't want to do it.

Sometimes we don't feel like doing something. We just lack motivation. Other times, we have a more emotional response that I call the "little kid syndrome." It feels like we're a 2 year old screaming, "I don't want to do that!"

Solution: Just "DO IT!"
When we're not sure why we don't want to do something, the first task is to figure out why. There might be a simple action you can take that allows you to move forward. An example might be you don't want to go to the library to study. Why? It's a long walk. Solution: take your favorite music to inspire you on your walk.

You can also think about what benefits you will get by accomplishing a task. Even as small a recognition as "If I do this then I won't feel so guilty" might inspire action. Sometimes it is just acknowledging that finishing the task at hand will pave the way for the thing you really want. Also check that you are attaching a personal value to the goal. Remember tapping into our personal values can provide motivation.

And sometimes, as NIKE says, we have to just "Do it."

Many times taking one small action we initially don't want to do can lead to motivation to complete a project. An example for me is this book. There were many instances where I did not want to sit at the computer and write. So I decided to just sit down and write one paragraph. Pretty soon, I was in the flow and inspired to write 2 more pages.

SUMMARY

So we have looked at a lot of ways to break through obstacles in creating the life of your dreams. It's always about, first, determining whether you are dealing with an external or internal obstacle. Then it's about addressing the obstacle. What actions need to be taken? What beliefs need to be changed?

Remember to ask for help from those who make you feel safe and supported. It can be helpful to have at least one person you tell your fears. This person can help keep you accountable by gently reminding you of your progress and encouraging you to continue on.

When you find fear creeping in, ask yourself, "Is this a rational or irrational fear?"

Keeping yourself accountable while remaining kind to yourself is the key to letting go of your fears. Being angry at yourself usually reinforces the fear. Acknowledge your fear and how it affects your life. Then take small steps to overcome it. This can release you from being fear's victim. Even if you do choose to keep a fear, knowing you have made a conscious choice to hold on to it may give you a new level of peace you did not have before.

Fear, in and of itself, is not a bad thing. It is a very natural response to danger. If we did not have fear, we would not survive. A part of us is warning that we need to be careful. That part only wants to protect us, make sure we are safe. The problem is when fear becomes an unnecessary and paralyzing hindrance.

Ultimately, you get to choose if you are going to allow fear to hold you back. As President Franklin D. Roosevelt said, *"The only thing we have to fear is fear itself."*

CHAPTER 6 – THE REST OF THE STORY...

When I first met Tony, I was taken aback by his presence. Standing over 6 feet tall, his deep booming voice filled my office. Tony was a high-powered, hard-working executive. He had always wanted to be successful in the corporate world and he had more than achieved that goal.

So why was he seeking my help?

Tony wasn't happy. Yes, he had created the life of his dreams. Professionally, he had envisioned exactly what he wanted, worked hard to achieve it and had conquered all the obstacles in the way. Personally, he had married his soul mate, a man of his dreams. It seemed like he had everything.

Yet something was missing...

I have partnered with a lot of clients on creating the life of their dreams. Using the process you have just learned, I have seen incredible transformations. Specificity in vision accompanied by goals tied into one's deepest values will produce extraordinary results. People can, literally, overhaul their lives if they want.

Sometimes, though, we aren't looking to overhaul our lives. Basically, we are pretty happy with them. Even so, we can fall back into old habits. We forget small things that helped us create the life of our dreams. Like our cars, our "timing" can get off. In these instances we need what I call a "Life Tune-Up." In short, it's just a reminder of things that allow us to be the best we can be.

And ultimately, isn't that what a dream life is all about?

GRATITUDE AS AN ATTITUDE

One of the most powerful things people can do for themselves is to be thankful. It is amazing how acknowledging and focusing on things we are grateful for can affect our lives. It can create positive feelings while tearing down walls built by fear, anger and hatred.

Gratitude is a choice. I have heard individuals say, "Sure, if I had what that person had, THEN I would be grateful." The truth is gratitude does not come with any set accumulation of things. It is consciously choosing to be thankful for those things you have no matter how small they may seem. One of the best things about gratitude is it is something you can choose anytime to feel more positive.

Some of the experiences clients have had are horrible. And I also know that if I allow my clients to stay stuck in the story of the "horribleness," the chances of them moving forward are slim. In this story is where people can build their emotional walls of fear, anger and hatred. Moving someone out of this negativity into gratitude can result in hope, love and acceptance.

When I am feeling down, my thoughts get caught in a loop. It's almost like I keep replaying, in my head, all the reasons why I'm in pain. I keep seeing myself as a victim. Just answering the question, "What am I grateful for, right now?" can break that loop. By having some thankfulness I begin to see my obstacles and myself differently. I begin to have hope, which usually inspires me to move past my hurdle. I become a "have" rather than a "have not." In being grateful, it's hard to stay stuck in the problem. I personally have never heard of anyone wanting to end it all because they were grateful.

EXERCISE #17: Gratitude

1. *GRATITUDE LIST*: Simply write down 20 things for which you are grateful. To build on this, encourage your friends and family to do their own lists. Agree to share them with each other when you are together.

2. *TOP THREE GRATITUDE LIST:* In the morning, just before you start your day, write down the top three things for which you are grateful. Then once an hour, take a moment to reflect back on what you are grateful for since the last time you wrote down your gratitude list. Look at your list and if the new item ranks in the top three, add it and adjust your list.

   Example: The top three things since waking up.
   1. My cat snuggling up next to me, purring.
   2. My favorite country song on the radio.
   3. Hot water for my shower. (Yesterday we only had cold water.)

   Next hour: Running for the train, I made it and, thus, I was on time for work. So my new list would look like.

   1. My cat snuggled up next to me, purring.
   2. My favorite country song on the radio.
   3. Made the 8:15 train.

   Since "making the train" was less than "my favorite county song" but more than "hot water for my shower," it replaces "hot water."

That night, when you go to bed, you will have your "Top Three" gratitude list. I do this anytime I feel depressed for an extended amount of time. This is a useful exercise because it gets us in the habit of being grateful. It makes us more alert to good things that are happening to us, things that could easily go unnoticed and underappreciated.

Living in gratitude changes how we experience the world. How? It changes the lenses through which we see our lives. Imagine if everyone lived in gratitude, searching for proof that their lives were amazing. Probably everyone would be a lot nicer to be around, thus causing more gratitude and it would just keep going.

When you wake up on the wrong side of the bed, when that deal at work falls through or when you miss your flight, stop and think of three things you are grateful for. No, it won't necessarily change the immediate situation but it will bring a little peace and happiness to your life. It's one way to stop and smell the roses.

IS EXCELLENCE ENOUGH?

"To improve is to change; to be perfect is to change often." – Winston Churchill

I worked with a really cool organization. They are considered one of the best in their field. I could see very little room for improvement. Neither could they. But that's not what the work was about. They wanted to go beyond being great and be greater.

As a coach and mediator, I usually work with clients who are trying to correct something. Rarely do I get called in to help them continue excelling. I think most of us grow from overcoming obstacles, building new skill sets or beliefs out of necessity.

So if everything is going great, why bother growing? It has been said, "That which does not grow, dies." Often we choose to grow or we will be forced to grow. An example might be a typewriter repairman from years past. His success would most certainly have dwindled in direct proportion to the rise of the computer if he did not change with the times.

One of the challenges of growing when things are "great" is figuring out what "greater" looks like. I suggest to clients that they look at others. Who is doing "greater" things and what, exactly, are they doing? What about them would they like to incorporate into their own lives?

Another way to find out what "greater" could be is to list your successes and then imagine what it would look like if you built on those. The aforementioned company's success had come from processes they had streamlined. Building on this, it occurred to them that they should share what they had done and to create a workbook to help others. From this, a new energy ignited the group. From an already energized group sprang an almost uncontainable excitement.

Once you discover what growth looks like, it is time to make a game plan to create it. What have you been doing that has already made you successful? How can you apply those skills or tactics to obtain your new goals?

The thing I do warn against is viewing your new goals as proof your current successes aren't worth celebrating. I have seen clients so excited about their achievements only to then get depressed when confronted with the idea of growing more. They view the idea that they can still grow as some sort of failure, almost as if anything less than perfection is not worth celebrating. Working towards that next level does not take away from your current greatness but enhances it. There will always be room for improvement.

I always want to continue growing. It is not necessarily to see how many goals I can accomplish but rather it's about experiences along the way. To me, it really is about the journey. It is about picking a place on the map, a goal, and then planning out the route to get there, emphasizing the choice to experience all the sights along the way. Once you have reached your goal, it is then making the decision that the journey isn't over. You get to pick a new goal, a new destination on the map, and start the process all over again. To me THAT is living.

30-DAY IMPROVEMENT CHALLENGE

As Abraham Maslow says, "You will either step forward into growth or you will step back into safety." A participant in one of my workshops asked: "If I commit to spend one hour a day for the next month on self-improvement, what would you suggest I do?"

What a great question!

Spending an hour a day doing something to improve yourself is perfect for a "personal tune-up!" And even if you didn't have an hour but only 15 to 30 minutes, you probably would see some nice changes.

So what do I suggest? Here are the Top 5 things that came to mind.

Journaling

Besides therapy and coaching, journaling is one of the best ways to get to know yourself. It helps me examine my thoughts and emotions. Journaling is also a great tool to be more creative. To use it to evaluate your life, simply write about your day. Concentrate on how you feel about the day's events. What questions do you have for yourself? On a scale of one to 10, how would you rate the day? If you had the chance to do something over, what would you do?

To increase your creativity, I suggest using a format Julia Cameron calls, "Artist's Pages." Write stream of consciousness for three pages. Write down anything and everything that comes to mind. Don't shortchange the length, either. When I do this exercise, my most creative and innovative ideas are usually found in the last third of the last page. Write continuously. There is no stopping to think or edit. The purpose is to write so fast your brain can't judge what you are writing. By making the mind give up judgment, you increase your creativity.

Meditation

There are a lot of ways to meditate and many of them fit nicely into a 30-day period.

If you are a novice at meditating, start small. Try different methods to see what works for you. There are meditations where you repeat a mantra over and over. These mantras can be anything from a single word like "love" or the sound "om" to a more complex phrase like "Om Mani Padme Hum" (meaning: jewel in the lotus). Some meditations involve simply staring at a candle and attempting to empty your mind. When your mind starts to wander, gently return your focus to the candle.

More advanced students might want to add more structure to their practice. I would suggest something like Deepak Chopra's 21-day Meditation Challenge. Another option would be to sign up for a 30-day meditation class. Or it might be a commitment to do your meditation consistently for 30 days. As an added challenge, take five minutes after each meditation to write down any realizations that you had.

Exercise

Make the commitment to start a 30-day exercise regimen.

This can be anything from simply walking 30 minutes a day to a more extensive workout you develop with the assistance of a trainer. There are also group exercise classes if you feel you need more inspiration or instruction. Convince a friend to take the class with you.

A couple of things to consider with exercise programs:

1. If you are at all unsure about whether you should be doing a particular exercise due to your health, talk to your doctor.

2. When exercising, it is important to take days off to rest your body. Injuries are more likely to occur if you exercise every day. You might consider meditating on your days off.

Reading

My father is a teacher and reads a lot. One thing he taught me is that you can't be the same after you read a book. For 30 days, commit to reading an hour a day. What books? Have friends suggest books. Maybe pick five self-help books that speak to you. Or read five books on five different types of religious practices or some other literature that presents conflicting views. The goal is to learn or explore things you don't know or necessarily agree with.

Something new

Try doing something new every day for 30 days. Make a list of 30 things, each of which could be done in an hour or less. If you feel like you have more time (say 3-6 hours) on some days, then make a list of things that might take longer. Map out a schedule on the calendar. A suggestion is to plan some events with a friend or group of friends. Sometimes when we get tired of things, connecting with others can renew our commitment.

One last idea is to think of a realistic goal that you can achieve in 30 days. This goal should be something that stretches but doesn't overwhelm you. It also shouldn't be something that is easy for you to achieve. Once you have that goal, go backwards and figure out what you need to have completed by the end of Week 1, Week 2 and Week 3 in order to be finished by the end of the month. Then plan to do some work each day toward reaching your weekly goal. After following this schedule for four weeks, you should be right at the finish line for your 30-day goal.

An example is training for a small race like a 5k. In order to build up to running the 5k, you will need to run small amounts on specific days, gradually increasing your distance until you are ready.

MAKE THE CHOICE TO LIVE

I was on the phone with my mother one night and she told me someone in our extended family died quite suddenly. She was at a function, went home, and the next morning she was dead.

I have to say that put my life in perspective.

Unfortunately, none of us are guaranteed how much time we have on this planet. One of my friends went to the gym and died suddenly on the treadmill, although he was only thirty-some years old. Another friend, diagnosed with terminal cancer, told me it's hard to plan for the future when you aren't supposed to have a future. She stopped living because she was too busy dying.

From a coaching perspective, two thoughts come to me about all this:

1. *How proud are you of the life you are living?* If you were attending your own funeral, what would you want others to say about you? What accomplishments, what things would you like to be remembered for? If you died today, are you happy with how your relationships stand? Are your resentments keeping you from connecting to those you love?

I hear over and over that when people are on their deathbed, resentments fade as their final goodbyes are said. I want people to remember me for the one-on-one moments they have encountered with me. I want them to say, because of those moments, their lives were changed for the better. This is something for me to remember when I am tired and grumpy on the bus, and the guy wants to engage me in a conversation. What an opportunity for me to live my purpose. When I do remember this and engage, I usually leave those encounters feeling rejuvenated and peaceful.

2. *Are you present for your own life?* We can tend to focus too much on the past or future instead of being in the moment. Life is about being awake and present.

Being up in our heads about the past or future is literally the same as living our lives in a virtual reality machine. The past is made up of memories clouded by our own interpretations of what really happened. The future we make up based on our hopes, expectations, and fears.

One particular weekend I went to a retreat. My experience started with running late for the bus on that Friday night. I then found myself nervous about who I would be rooming with and what kind of exercises we might be doing that might leave me feeling vulnerable. I hardly remember anything about that first night. I was anything but present. The first exercise Saturday morning was to go outside, breathe and get present. As I did this, I was suddenly slammed into the present moment.

What an amazing experience! The leaves were changing. My breath was almost taken away by the surprise of discovering such beauty. Finally I was present. And what a "present" I got!

Not sure how to go about doing the above? I have heard that a lot of terminally ill people get clarity around the meaning of their lives when they receive their diagnosis. The report is that, for many, the struggle for money and success suddenly disappears. Their priorities simplify and usually center on people in their lives. For them, it becomes about savoring the moment.

How would your life change if you knew you had only three months to live? What are you putting off till tomorrow that you could do today?

COURAGE TO BE YOUR AUTHENTIC SELF

Originality—it's something that most of us applaud when we see it, but are too scared to do ourselves.

It can be risky to be original. What will people say? If the wheel isn't broken, why fix it? It's probably just safer to do what we know.

Our movie and live theater choices are great examples of this philosophy. We're seeing a record number of movie remakes. Most of the current Broadway shows are remounts of past successes or popular movies that have been turned into musicals. I guess I can't fault the producers. One flop could ruin them for life. It's become too risky to be original.

But my question is: What are the dangers of *not* being our authentic selves?

I see many clients who are pondering their life purpose. Along with this, they are looking for fulfillment. When I ask them about their passions, what makes them feel alive, many are stumped. It's almost like they've forgotten. They're caught up in being someone else for the sake of emotional safety and sometimes, in extreme cases, physical safety.

One example might be the person letting go of her artistic self in order to have a great paying job. Another might be the person who hides his sexuality so he won't disappoint or lose the love of his family.

My observations of others, and myself, suggest that there usually comes a time when not being ourselves becomes too much. We've forgotten who we are, or why we started doing what we're doing in the first place. Playing a role that is not authentic causes much misery.

The risk of not being our authentic selves is that we lose ourselves. When we lose that, we often feel hatred—towards others for doing what we would love to be doing, or being what we would like to be, and towards ourselves for putting ourselves last.

Here are considerations to help find our authentic selves:

- *Safety*: Virtually everyone needs to feel safe. In exploring our authentic selves, it's important to do it with people who love and support us. Especially at the beginning, the expression of our originality, our creativity, is quite fragile. Even one misspoken criticism can cause us to go back into hiding.
- *Try new things*: Think you might like kick boxing? Do a class. Remember as a kid that you loved to sing? Join a choir. Try to shake up your daily routine.
- *Welcome not being perfect*: It's important to give yourself permission to be imperfect. When trying shoes on, some just aren't going to fit. And when you find the right shoes, they feel all that much better after having tried on ones that don't.
- *Be your own best friend*: When you do connect to your authentic self, guard it with your life. Literally. Remember, not everyone will be happy with your journey, either because they are finding your relationship with them is changing because you're "different," or because they're secretly jealous,

wanting to find their own authentic self. If and when this happens, don't let those people deter you.

Originality often fails - at first.

Many times it is individuals who aren't afraid to be themselves that are the most successful. Oprah Winfrey, Steve Jobs, Walt Disney, J.K. Rowling, Madonna, Jerry Seinfeld, Truman Capote, Robert Redford, Bob Dylan and even Elvis were all originally told they had no talent and that they should give up. Yet, by sticking to their original, authentic selves, they all, literally, changed the world.

FORGIVENESS

A common stumbling block for clients is resentments. Holding on to past hurts can make it almost impossible to move forward no matter how specific your vision or dedication to a great action plan may be. The solution: Forgiveness.

I can almost hear some of you laughing, saying, "Oh, THAT'S all."

Forgiveness is difficult and seems to be a challenge for most of us. That must be why there are literally hundreds of books on the subject.

Forgiveness: What is it? Why is it so important? How do we do it? One dictionary says it is "to give up resentment of or claim to requital for" or "to cease to feel resentment against." Resentments can take away a person's life. Instead of pursuing those things that bring us joy, resentments keep us prisoner by having us replay the wrongs we have experienced. Hours, days and years of this repetition cause bitterness and negativity.

But the thought of forgiving or "letting the person off the hook" often seems inconceivable to us. Forgiving is not for the other person. It is for the one with the resentment. Forgiveness restores peace of mind by changing the way a situation is perceived. I think the biggest fear is that forgiving means denying or forgetting something happened. It is not. It actually is acknowledging what happened and then looking at it in a way that can bring peace to the victim.

Three-Step Forgiveness Process:

1. *Acknowledge:* Write down both the hard, cold facts of the situation and *all* the feelings you have regarding the facts. Remember facts are just what happened with no emotion. The facts can't be disputed because they just are. It's also important to acknowledge when you are not sure of the facts. In regard to feelings, anger and hatred, of course, need to be addressed but also what you are afraid will happen if you forgive.

   I find it is extremely important to acknowledge our part in the conflict. Another thing to consider is that people react to our actions. What, if anything, did you possibly do to cause someone's actions? Forgiveness might be as simple as acknowledging that what happened is in the past yet we are still holding on to it.

2. *Decide:* Ask yourself what is the payoff for holding on to this resentment. Assess the pros and cons of forgiving this person. How would your life change if you let go of this resentment? How would you be free? Finally, after you have spelled this out, consciously decide if you want to forgive.

3. *Change*: If you decide that you do want to forgive, you have already started on step 3 and the process of change. So what are we changing? We are *not* trying to change history. What's done is done. We *are* trying to change what is within our control which is our

perception. An example of this might be in forgiving your parents. The facts are they yelled, worked long hours and generally put you down. You resent your parents because you feel they didn't love you enough. What are other ways of looking at this? Well, they worked long hours to try to pay the bills so you would have food and shelter. When they yelled or got angry at you, it might be because they didn't know how to communicate their fears lovingly to you. Their parents may have yelled at them also. And then you put yourself in their shoes. How well would you do if you were raising six children on less than you earn now? You realize perhaps they weren't doing it the best way possible but they were doing the best they could at that given moment.

Forgiveness can be one of the most challenging things we can do. Professional help may be needed to assist with this process. Don't judge yourself for seeking help. Time is needed to walk through the hurt. Don't judge yourself if it doesn't happen overnight. And sometimes forgiveness seems impossible. Don't beat yourself up if you get overwhelmed. I was once abused by a person I believed didn't deserve my forgiveness. To forgive him was to let him off the hook and I was not going to do that. Then the thought occurred, with professional help, I was actually abusing myself as much or more than this man had abused me. The offense took place years before, but I was still reliving the horror by continuing to judge him. The man was dead. He was done abusing me. I, though, was still being abused daily ... by my own thoughts. After that, I decided I was ready to forgive.

Holding on to anger is like grasping a hot coal with the intent of throwing it at someone else; you are the one who gets burned. — Buddha

SAYING 'YES' TO 'NO'

A friend of mine was telling me how his almost 2-year-old daughter had a new favorite word: "NO!" I loved it. In fact, as we parted, I was wishing some of my clients could get more comfortable saying the word "no." What is the challenge in saying this simple word?

Saying "yes" when one really should say "no" can create a lot of stress. An example is when "yes" means we are over-committing ourselves. Why do we do this? Any number of reasons from we don't want to be (or appear) selfish in not helping, to we don't want someone else to feel burdened by our "no." Consequently, sometimes the quality goes down in everything we are doing because we simply have too much work to do.

But if we said "no" in this instance, one might look at this as an opportunity to allow more time and energy to honor those things that already have our "yes." We would be providing better quality by limiting the quantity. And everyone would win. Really? Well, we win by not stressing ourselves out. The prior commitments win because they can have 100 percent of our attention and we are not stressed. And the person we said "no" to is free to find someone who can give a 100 percent "yes" to them.

Here are some great tips (modified from a Staff publication at the Mayo Clinic) on figuring out when to say "no":

- Figure out your priorities.
  - Is this new commitment important to you?
  - Yes? Do it.
  - No? Don't do it.
- Ask "To stress or not to stress?"
  - How much stress will be added to your life by saying "yes?"

- Is this stress something you can live with and not create resentments towards yourself or others?
- Plead "Not Guilty"
  - How much is guilt playing a part in your saying "yes?"
  - If you let go of the guilt and did what you really wanted to do, what would be your answer then?
- Mull it over
  - Not 100 percent sure of what to say? Wait. Rarely does waiting an hour or even a night to give an answer create negative consequences. *But* I have seen clients in pure hell for answering right away and then almost immediately realizing they should have said the opposite.

The next challenge can sometimes be actually saying "no." How does one do it?

- Use direct language (like the word, "no"). The goal here is to avoid mixed messages like "I think..." or "I'm pretty sure..."
- Be specific and brief in your explanation. Avoid justifying your answer or getting into a conversation that might lead to saying "yes."
- Tell the truth. Avoid making up reasons. If the truth does come out later it can have negative consequences on your relationship. Plus, being honest validates you and your choices.
- Be positive. Try to affirm the person or group and what they are doing. This way there is an opportunity for them to feel supported even though you are saying "no" to their specific request.
- Hold your ground. After you have made your decision, calmly stick to your "no" if it is challenged. If you feel a

change of heart coming on, remember you can always say something like, "Perhaps I do need to reconsider. Let me take some more time to think about your request." The important thing, though, is *not* to say an automatic "yes."

When you say "no," be prepared for some people to be disappointed. That is OK and does not mean you are doing anything wrong. If you truly want to help, brainstorm ways that the current request could be changed to fit both their needs and yours.

FIND BALANCE AND AVOID BURNOUT

I have a confession to make: I get tired. I get cranky. I get tired of working. I get burnt out. This is pretty common for those of us trying to make our lives better. To my clients who are experiencing burn-out, I suggest the following:

1. *Why*? First look for the reasons for your burnout. Consider how much you are working. Have you scheduled yourself too thin? Are you overwhelmed by all the expectations that have been placed on you by yourself or others? Perhaps there is an easy fix of letting go of some of the things that seem to be burning you out. If you can't let go of them completely, try seeing if you can take a break from them for awhile.

2. *Sleep*: Are you getting enough sleep? I am amazed how many people don't get adequate sleep. If I don't get enough sleep, my crankiness is exacerbated. When you feel burnt out my suggestion is to make sure you are getting at least eight hours per night. Also try to be consistent by going to sleep around the same time each night.

3. *Stillness:* Stop and be still. This might be for a few hours or even, if possible, days. No, I don't mean plan

an extensive vacation putting more stress into your life. A break means you stop and relax. This is a time to reflect. Sometimes, when I get to this point, I go to a silent retreat center to be with myself silently for 24 hours. No TV. No email. No phone ... just me.

4. *Free your mind:* During times like these, meditation is usually a sure way to release some of the pressure. This is along the same lines of No. 3 (stillness) but for a shorter period of time. Try meditating first thing in the morning when you wake up. This is a great way to get in a good frame of mind for the rest of the day. Also, when that burnt out feeling hits, take a couple of moments to disengage from your current situation and re-center by meditating. Even 2-3 minutes can be a mood changer.

5. *Lighten up:* Plan some time away from your usual routine and do something fun! When I suggest this, some clients inform me they are too busy to do this, that their life would fall apart. Imagine if your burnout gets so extreme you just say "f— it" and walk away from everything. The fallout would be greater than not rescheduling or cancelling a meeting or two. The pressure valve has to be released one way or another.

6. *Good, clean living:* When feeling burnt out, be aware of the foods you eat and the amount of exercise you get. Up the fruits and veggies. Cut back on the meats and processed foods. In regards to exercise, increase your cardio to get those endorphins going.

I am the type who loves to go and go. My mother says I burn the candle at both ends. It's hard for me to resist. The adrenaline rush I get from a busy schedule and contact with lots of people is invigorating. Unfortunately, when I or anybody else does this, we are headed for burnout. My experience has been that my burnout starts off with mental stress and then, if I don't stop, the physical stress catches up and I am sick and down for the count.

To summarize the suggestions above, the solution for burnout is finding and implementing balance back into your life. In my case, I need to balance the busy parts of my life with time for stillness and rest. It's amazing how my attitude toward life changes when I do this.

"Happiness is not a matter of intensity but of balance, order, rhythm and harmony." — Thomas Merton

WHAT'S THE POINT?

You only get one life. This is it. This very moment is the first of the rest of your life. Ultimately, you get to choose how you will live those moments.

"A life lived in fear is a life half-lived." Spanish Proverb

You can wait. Wait for the right answers. Wait for the perfect idea to start working. Wait for the perfect partner before you start dating. Wait until your children are grown to start doing what you want. Wait until your death bed to start forgiving...

Or you can act now. Start saying "Yes!" to life.

Many of us say a strong "maybe" in regard to our lives:

> *Maybe I'll try that class.*
> *Maybe I'll take that trip.*
> *Maybe I'll quit my job and start doing what I REALLY love...*

I get it. The "maybe" seems safer, for we can say we are open and willing to make that change while always having an out. This is the deal, pure and simple. Success is rarely created out of maybes.

Say "Yes!" to:

- *Dreaming Big-* It costs nothing and is 100% safe.
- *Forgiving-* They may not deserve it but you do.
- *Getting Help-* We can't and shouldn't know everything. Asking for help gives us the necessary assistance for improving our lives AND it keeps us from being disconnected from others. Then we don't feel so alone.
- *Helping Others-* It has been said we keep what we give away. Being of service to others, of course, gives something to our fellow humans and also provides us with esteem and character building opportunities
- *Being Grateful-* It makes life more enjoyable by causing us to focus on the positive and to count our blessings.
- *Having Fun!!!-* No one gets out of this world alive so don't take it all so seriously. Enjoy life. Go dance in the rain...

In improvisation, a general rule is when a scene partner gives you a suggestion, take the suggestion and add to it. It is called "Yes, and..." An example might be if my scene partner said to me, "Hey bro, what's mom cooking?" I don't want to say, "I'm not your brother." That would stop the scene. Instead I would take his "suggestion" of being his brother and add to it like "Well, I'm not sure what mom is cooking but I know I haven't seen the cat in two days..."

Life is the same. What if we took what the Universe gave us and said "Yes, and..." to it? Half of success is just showing up and taking advantage of the opportunities presented. A lot of times, though, I watch people say "no" to the universe.

Start saying "Yes, and..." to life. This means being grateful and accepting life. Then it's about adding to your life by dreaming big and setting goals to get the most out of your life.

Many times, the dying say it's the chances they didn't take that cause some of their biggest regrets.

Still feel stuck? Here are some things that make up my dream life. Feel free to borrow from these until you have your own....

1. Live fearlessly
2. Laugh
3. Love
4. Give back
5. Hug
6. Give compliments
7. Seek out new experiences
8. Sleep late with a loved one
9. Be spontaneous
10. Be grateful
11. Read
12. Listen to music
13. Hold babies
14. Love a pet
15. Listen to children
16. Go to museums
17. Be active/play sports
18. Dance
19. Sing
20. Enjoy silence
21. Let others be right
22. Enjoy when you have to wait
23. Trust the universe
24. Do one thing you are afraid of every day (even as small as saying hi to a stranger)
25. Say I love you to those who matter to you
26. When people want to give, graciously take
27. Eat desserts at least once a week
28. Say I love you to yourself in the mirror
29. Secretly give to someone in need
30. Volunteer
31. Get out of debt
32. Forgive quickly
33. Go "offline" by shutting off your computer and phone for a period of time

34. Get comfortable saying "I need help'

35. Be ok with being wrong

36. Stop negative self-talk

37. Stop gossiping

38. Stop judging others

39. When you mess up, forgive yourself

40. Celebrate your "un" perfection (learn to laugh at yourself)

41. Give compliments- a lot

42. Try to do one thing better each day

43. Take a daily inventory. Those things you do well- keep doing. Ineffective things- stop or work on changing

44. If you have an addiction to anything admit it, seek help and have faith it will get better

45. Embrace relationships that support you. Let go of those that bring you down or bring you chaos

46. Get a coach or a therapist if you have deeper issues

47. Commit to "feel your feelings" and not avoid them

48. Be in awe, be impressed

49. Celebrate others

50. Stop being so hard on yourself

51. See your perfection

52. Stop being self-centered and start being us-centered

53. Thank your parents

54. Thank your children

55. Show respect to every human whether they deserve it or not

56. Respect life. Don't hurt or kill anything if you can help it (even if you think they deserve it)

57. Be creative every day

58. Act like a grownup but create like a child

59. Have a best friend. Have two...

60. Celebrate everything

61. Live moderately

62. Be of Service

63. Give others the benefit of the doubt until they prove you wrong

64. Trust the process

65. Do something nice for yourself every day.

66. When angry, don't make any sudden moves. Wait to speak

67. If unsure, sleep on major decisions

68. Ask people questions about themselves

69. See the world through a child's eyes

70. Lay out under the stars

71. Try to get to an ocean at least once a year

72. Set yearly goals

73. Go to a playground and swing

74. Learn your family history

75. Walk in the rain without an umbrella

76. Walk instead of driving or public transportation

77. Plan a surprise party for a friend or loved one

78. Take bubble baths

79. If in doubt, go with your gut

80. Stop trying to please everyone

A FINAL THOUGHT...

Not feeling the best about your life? Remembering your "ABC's" might help...

- A-Acceptance- We can't change the past but we can choose how we proceed.
- B- Believe- Have faith that things will work out.
- C-Confidence- Know you can do it.
- D-Decision- Choose to be happy.
- E- Efficiency- Let go of self-imposed blocks to arrive at your goals quicker.
- F-Fun- Laugh. A lot.
- G-Goals- Set realistic goals and review them often to make sure they are taking you where you want to go.
- H- Health- You only have one body- use it wisely.
- I- Integrity- When faced with doing something not in alignment with who you are just to get ahead, don't do it.
- J- Joy- Try to find the joy in every moment.
- K – Knowledge- As my dad said, you can never go wrong with learning. Learn as much as you can.
- L- Love yourself- Celebrate yourself- a lot!
- M- Meditation- Quiet the mind to hear the Universe speak.
- N- "No"- Learn to honor yourself by the ability to say 'no' to things that don't resonate with you. This is part of being efficient in your life.
- O- Open-mindedness- Usually there is more than one way to look at something.
- P- Perseverance- Don't give up. If one door closes, look for an open window.
- Q- Quality- When faced with a choice, choose quality over quantity in all parts of your life.
- R- Respond vs. react- Instead of reacting with anger, learn to pause and respond. The result will be less regrets.

- S- Silence- Learn to be quiet. Sometimes the most beautiful moments are in the silence.
- T- Thankfulness- Gratitude decreases depression.
- U- Unapologetic – Be the best parts of you, not apologizing for the things that make you unique.
- V- Values- Live by those values that are most important to you.
- W- Win-win- In conflict, try to abandon self-centered fear and think of how everyone might "win."
- X- Xerox- Find the people you want to be like and perhaps "copy" their path. Don't re-invent the wheel.
- Y- "Yes"- Say "Yes" to life. No one gets out alive so live it up!
- Z- Zero excuses- Take full responsibility for where you are and make the appropriate choices to get to where you want to be. Let go of being the victim in your life and embrace being the hero.

"Life is simple, it's just not easy." ~Author Unknown

About the Author

Bob Kiser is a successful author, speaker, coach and mediator. His mission is to help clients let go of fear to embody who they really want to be. This gentle process creates sustainable change by building a strong foundation on the client's own strengths and uniqueness. Whether working with an individual, couple or corporation, Bob's clients end their time with him feeling empowered.

Bob has been a speaker for a variety of national and international audiences. He is known for his highly interactive presentations that leave audiences charged and motivated. He also conducts workshops for smaller groups on more specific obstacles. Motivation, fear-busting and conflict resolution are just a few of his most popular topics.

Besides his private practice, Bob also serves as the Associate Director of the Graham Clinical Performance Center in the Department of Medical Education at the University of Illinois @ Chicago. The center provides simulated clinical experiences for medical students and residents that focus on communication and interpersonal skill building. He is also a mediator for UIC through the Office of Access and Equity.

He received his certifications from the Institute for Professional Excellence in Coaching (iPEC) and the Center for Conflict Resolution (CCR).

www.bobkisercoaching.com

Made in the USA
Lexington, KY
02 September 2018